Forty Days
&
Forty Nights

A Guide to Finding God's Peace,
One Day at a Time

LOUIS AND KIERA DESCHAMPS

For more information, visit https://www.kdconsults.com/
Kiera DesChamps
CEO/Founder KD Consulting Group, LLC

Photo of James DesChamps taken at Oak Island, North Carolina
Photo of Hunter DesChamps taken at Hanging Rock, North Carolina

ISBN: 979-8-9995485-2-8 (paperback)
ISBN: 979-8-9995485-3-5 (hardcover)

Library of Congress Control Number: 2025917817

Cover Design by Kelly Nielsen
Interior Design by Amit Dey

DEDICATION

To our sons, James and Hunter DesChamps,

This devotional spans over thirty years of our life experiences and stories, and you've been part of it all. From the answered prayers to the lost jobs, from financial struggles and marriage challenges to emotional pain and unexpected blessings— you were there. You lived through our mistakes, witnessed our vulnerabilities, and celebrated our wins. Through it all, you loved us with a grace that only God could have taught you.

Thank you for your patience as the four of us grew up together. Thank you for walking this road with us—even when it was hard, confusing, or uncertain. Your love, support, and faithfulness have been steady reminders of God's goodness and provision.

We dedicate our very first book to you!

We wrote it to remind you—again and again—of who God is and always will be. You've seen Him show up for us over and over. And now, it's your turn to walk boldly into your own journey with Jesus at the center and share it with your families.

He's done it before—and He will surely do it again.

Love, Mommy and Daddy

TABLE OF CONTENTS

FOREWORD

There is a rhythm to the life of faith that often reflects the wilderness. Forty days in the desert. Forty nights of rain. Forty days of testing, waiting, or preparing. Throughout Scripture, God uses these periods not to punish but to form individuals. They are times of pruning, recalibrating, and awakening—a divine invitation to turn away from distraction and draw near again to the One who restores the soul.

This devotional, *Forty Days and Forty Nights*, serves as one such invitation. Louis and Kiera DesChamps have crafted a journey that is honest and filled with personal stories and rich scriptural truths. It provides space for reflection, repentance, and authentic communion with God.

But more than anything, it reminds us of a central truth we dare not forget:

> **Every true revival—whether in a person's heart or throughout a congregation—begins with intentional, immersive, and intensive prayer.**

From the upper room in Acts to historical spiritual awakenings and the quiet, unseen breakthroughs in your living room, revival never happens by chance. It is nurtured. Not earned, but received through humility, hunger, and sincere prayer. This kind of prayer is more than just words spoken to God—it's time spent with Him. It's surrender. It's listening. It's waiting.

I believe that what most of us need isn't more information, but more immersion—whether in God's Word, in God's presence, or in communities that come together until change happens.

That's what makes this forty-day journey so meaningful. It's a chance to immerse yourself in prayer, not superficial, quick devotionals, but intentional time set aside for God to work deeply.

You may enter these forty days feeling tired, uncertain, stuck, or spiritually numb. That's okay. The first miracle is just showing up. Bring your weariness. Bring your questions. Bring your heart, no matter what it is.

God meets us not in our ideal selves, but in our real condition, and He revives us from there.

My prayer is that these devotionals not only encourage you but also ignite a fire within you. That they stir up a new hunger and awaken in you a strong desire to seek God, not just sometimes, but urgently. That through Scripture, prayer, and reflection, your heart would be wholly focused on Him.

May these next forty days become a sacred space and serve not just as a devotional journey, but also as an opportunity for a daily encounter with the Living God.

—*Sergio Quevedo*

INTRODUCTION

We've lived through the storms.

The seasons of grief, loss, financial hardship, unanswered questions, broken relationships, and unexpected changes. We've had nights filled with tears, days when prayers felt like whispers into the wind, and years where hope seemed like it was taking its time to show up. But through it all—*we're still here.*

This devotional is not written from a place of theory or surface-level encouragement. It's written from the depths of real experience. Over thirty years of walking with God through joy and sorrow, mistakes and miracles, setbacks, and victories. This collection of reflections, scriptures, and prayers comes from the heart of two people who have been through the fire and can say with confidence: *God is faithful.*

We believe that God allows certain tests in our lives not to break us, but to strengthen us. He knows that even when it hurts, we will pray harder, trust deeper, and tell more people about His goodness. He trusts us with trials because He knows we'll testify. Our lives are living proof that pain has purpose, and that the same God who brought us through before will do it again.

If you find yourself in a difficult season—questioning your direction, your strength, or even your faith—this devotional is for you. These forty days are designed to walk with you through the wilderness and into the arms of God's peace, one step, one scripture, and one prayer at a time.

So come as you are. Broken or whole, weary or hopeful. There's room for you here. And there's a God who is ready to meet you—right where you are.

—Louis & Kiera DesChamps

DAY 1:

LORD, DID YOU REMEMBER ME?

Scripture: Psalms 37:23-25

"The Lord makes firm the steps of the one who delights in him;
though they may stumble, they will not fall, for the Lord upholds them
with his hand."

Introduction

It's natural to look back and reflect on the experiences that shaped us over the past twelve months. In looking back, you may find times when you experienced both blessings and challenges, moments of joy, and times of struggle. Each experience offers us a chance to see God's hand at work in our lives.

The Journey Begins

At the start of the year, many of us set goals—spiritual aspirations, health commitments, and dreams for the future. We envisioned a year of growth, filled with meaningful moments and accomplishments— a new job, a new degree, or new relationships. Yet, as the months unfolded, we often faced unexpected challenges: job losses, health scares, relational strains, and moments that tested our faith. In these trying times, it can be easy to feel abandoned or forgotten. During these times, I find myself asking, "*Where did You go, Lord?*" In the midst of my challenges and feelings of abandonment, my loneliness makes me question His presence. Once I reflect, I have to remember that God never leaves us. Even in our darkest moments, He is there, holding us close.

Choosing to remember His goodness is a powerful act of faith. It shifts our focus from our struggles to God's faithfulness. When we intentionally recall His goodness, we can find peace amidst chaos.

Consider moments from your year that highlighted God's faithfulness:

- Job Loss: Perhaps you faced an unexpected job loss, feeling uncertain about the future. Yet, as you look back, you may recognize how God provided a new opportunity that aligned more closely with your passions. I have had my share of job losses, which quickly became blessings.
- Family Reunions: If you experienced estrangement from a loved one, reflect on the joy of reconnection and healing, seeing God's hand in restoration. You may not want to hear this, but in these moments, God is usually growing us.
- Personal Growth: Think about the lessons learned through trials. How did they shape you? What strengths emerged that you didn't know you had? I know, I know, it's easier said than done, but it's so true! Psalm 77:11-14 reminds us, "I will remember the deeds of the Lord; yes, I will remember your miracles of long ago."
- As you prepare for the year ahead, even if it's already started, take a moment to declare what you remember about God's faithfulness.

- His Goodness: His goodness chases after us, even when we feel unworthy. Can you imagine being chased down for love?

- Strength in Waiting: One of my favorite songs asks the question about what we do while we are waiting on God.

- Waiting drives me crazy, and I am always trying to find things to distract me and keep me busy. However, God reminds me to worship, even if I don't have any words to say. "But they that wait upon the Lord shall renew their strength" (Isaiah 40:31).

- Joy Will Come: Don't you just hate when you're in the midst of mourning, depression, and doubt, someone tells you that joy will come? I want to experience that joy right now. "Weeping may endure for a night, but joy comes in the morning (Psalm 30:5)."

- If God is for Us: "If God is for us, who can be against us?" (Romans 8:31).

Personal Reflection

1. Journaling: Write down specific instances where you saw God at work in your life this past year. Reflect on how these experiences shaped your faith.

   _____

   _____

   _____

2. Share Your Story: Consider sharing your experiences with a friend or a group. Your testimony might inspire others to recognize God's hand in their own lives.

3. Prayer: Spend time in prayer, thanking God for His faithfulness and asking for strength to face the new year with hope and courage.

Conclusion

As you move forward in the days and months, let's carry these memories with us. Let's be intentional about sharing our testimonies, encouraging one another in faith, and spreading the hope that comes from remembering God's faithfulness. Know that, of course, He remembers you!

PRAYER

Heavenly Father, thank You for Your constant presence and faithfulness throughout the year. Help me to remember the ways You have worked in my life, even amidst the trials. As I step into the days ahead, help me to carry these memories with me, trusting in Your plans for my future. Bless me as I seek to honor You in all I do. In Jesus' name, Amen.

DAY 2:

REVIVE: A SPIRITUAL CPR

Scripture: Psalms 119:25

"My soul clings to the dust; revive me according to Your word."

Introduction

I watched a movie based on a true story about a young teenager who fell through ice and was submerged under freezing cold water for twenty minutes. It took many medical rescuers, experts, and prayers to save and bring this boy back to life. All I could think about was whether I was drowning or unconscious, could I be revived?

Have you ever felt spiritually lifeless—like you're gasping for breath, overwhelmed by circumstances, weighed down by anxiety, or drained by life's struggles? Just as CPR is performed to restore physical life, God offers us spiritual CPR to revive our weary souls. When we feel like we are barely holding on, He is ready to breathe new life into us.

Spiritual Revival

There was a time when I felt completely drained, like I was on auto-pilot—doing what needed to be done but feeling no real connection to God. The daily routines of life became robotic. Anxiety gripped my thoughts, making me question my purpose and ability to move forward. I was overwhelmed, clinging to my own strength instead of allowing God to revive me.

Much like a person in need of cardiopulmonary resuscitation, CPR, I needed divine intervention. Christ-Powered Revival, CPR, reminds us that God is our life source, and He alone can restore what is broken.

In Psalms 119:25, the psalmist cries out, "My soul clings to the dust; revive me according to Your word." This is an honest admission of spiritual exhaustion, but also a declaration of faith. When we feel life-less, God's Word is the breath that restores us, the pulse that brings us back to life, and the strength that helps us stand again.

When a person undergoes CPR, the rescuer follows a precise process to restore life. Spiritually, we also need steps to be revived:

1. Check the Heart (Examine Yourself) – In physical CPR, we first check for signs of life. Spiritually, we must ask: Where have I grown distant from God? What has been weighing me down? Am I prioritizing His presence?

2. Clear the Airway (Remove Spiritual Blockages) – Just as CPR requires clearing obstructions for proper breathing, we must remove anything that hinders our connection with God—doubt, fear, distractions, or unconfessed sin.

3. Breathe in the Word (Take in Scripture and Prayer) – In CPR, breath is given to restore oxygen to the body. Spiritually, we need the breath of God through His Word and prayer to revive our souls.

4. Restore the Pulse (Take Action) – A revived life requires movement. Worship, serving others, and stepping out in faith all restore our spiritual pulse.

Now, take a deep breath. Inhale and exhale slowly.

Personal Reflection

1. Identify areas in your life where you feel spiritually weak or distant from God.

   _____

   _____

2. Remove distractions and carve out intentional time for God.

3. Meditate on scripture, worship, and spend time in prayer.

4. Instead of relying on yourself, lean on God for renewal.

5. Join a faith-based community, serve others, or take a step of faith in an area where you've hesitated.

Conclusion

Just as CPR revives a struggling heart, God's Word breathes new life into our weary souls. When we feel spiritually lifeless, crushed by burdens, or distant from Him, He stands ready to restore us. Psalm 119:25 reminds us, _"I am laid low in the dust; preserve my life according to your word."_ Our revival begins when we return to His presence, allowing His truth to renew our minds and His Spirit to strengthen our hearts.

If you feel like your faith is gasping for air, remember: God is the ultimate Rescuer. Call on Him. Breathe in His promises. Let Him revive your soul, bringing you back to a place of purpose, passion, and unwavering trust in Him.

Will you allow God to perform spiritual CPR on your heart today?

PRAYER

Lord, I come before You feeling weary, in need of Your life-giving breath. My soul clings to the dust, but I know that You are my source of revival. Clear away anything that blocks my connection with You. Fill me with Your presence and restore my strength. Help me to press forward, trusting that You are breathing new life into me. Thank You for being my source of renewal. In Jesus' name, Amen.

DAY 3:

GOD IS STILL IN CHARGE (I HAVE PLANS FOR YOU)

Scripture: Jeremiah 29:11

"For I know the plans I have for you," declares the LORD,
"plans to prosper you and not to harm you, plans to give you hope
and a future."

Introduction

Have you ever found yourself stuck and wondering, *what am I doing with my life? There has to be something better than where I am now. This job can't be it for me.*

God has a plan for each of us. The problem is that we want to be in control. We think that we know what is best. We find ourselves in so much unnecessary trouble because we want to be in control. If only we learn to just let God lead us and trust Him.

Finding True Success

A few years ago, a friend told me that God had something greater planned for my life beyond my current job. I was excited because God had finally heard my prayers. For the next year, I would feel this stirring in my spirit, a sense that God was up to something significant. Yet, there was no change. I was still stuck in the same job. Although I felt this strong impression that my time in my job was limited and my life was about to change.

Have you ever felt that way? Discontent in your job, situation or relationship, yet you're not sure what's next? I performed my job to the best of my ability, but I knew in my heart that there was something more. It wasn't until a year and a half later that a simple invitation to help a friend paint his new home would alter my life. It was from that job that I was encouraged to start my own business. After praying, seeking clarity and direction, I started a handyman business that later became a lawn care business.

Why does the Bible compare the devil to a lion? 1 Peter 5:8 says, *"The devil walks about like a roaring lion, seeking whom he may devour."* Did you know that a lion's roar can be heard up to five miles away, serving as an alert of its presence? It's meant to instill fear and cause us to run in the opposite direction. But what if we chose to rest in the presence of God instead? What would that look like? Ask Daniel how he fared in the lion's den. What about the three Hebrew boys who stood firm in their faith? Remember Job, who said, "Though He slay me, yet will I trust in Him." Job's faith was rewarded with blessings twice as great as before.

To succeed in an enterprise or activity, to achieve economic success, and to live and experience the fullness of God—peace, joy, and freedom from worry— we must remain focused on God and trust His plan for our lives. The enemy loves to distract us with doubts and fears.

Personal Reflection

As you seek to cultivate your relationship with God, consider these vows as a commitment to your spiritual journey:

1. Will you dedicate yourself with a whole heart to allow Jesus to be your guide?

   _____

   _____

2. Will you cultivate your relationship with Him, trusting in His provision for both eternal salvation and your daily needs?

   _____

   _____

3. Will you commit to praying daily?

   _____

   _____

Conclusion

God truly has plans for each of us, and even when life feels uncertain, we can rest assured that He is still in charge. Embrace the freedom that comes with trusting in His perfect plan. Walk boldly into your future, knowing that where you place your faith, He will guide you every step of the way.

PRAYER

As I look around the world and things seem scary, thank you for reminding me that you are still in control. As I seek you more and more, please make it clear to me the plans that you have for my life. If I am not walking the path that you want me on, please gently correct me.

DAY 4:

HOW TO JUMP START A DEAD BATTERY

Scripture: Isaiah 40:31

"But those who wait on the LORD shall renew their strength; they shall mount up with wings like eagles, they shall run and not be weary, they shall walk and not faint."

Introduction

Have you ever gotten in your car, turned the key, only to hear a pitiful click? Your heart sinks as you realize the battery is dead. Sometimes, it gives you a warning—a flickering dashboard light or a slow cranking engine. Other times, it just leaves you stranded. I remember a particularly frustrating day, sitting in my car, trying repeatedly to start it. Each attempt drained the battery further, and after a while, all I could do was step out and look at my vehicle with despair.

The Power Source

I walked around the car, kicked the tires, and finally popped the hood—an instinctive sign of distress. As I touched the battery posts, I remembered the jumper cables I had tucked away. But I needed another source, another vehicle or a device that is capable of starting my car. I needed more power.

Just like my car, sometimes our spirits need a jump-start. If only there were a way to jump-start my spirit. I remember asking God how I recharge my drained spirit. He quickly responded, "Pray." Just open your mouth. Prayer is the jumper cable for your spirit.

Remember Mark 11:24: "Therefore I tell you, whatever you ask for in prayer, believe that you have received it, and it will be yours." Prayer invites God's power into your life, reviving your spirit.

Once you have prayed, it's time to wait on Him. The Bible reminds us that those who wait on the Lord shall mount up with wings like eagles. Did you know an eagle's wingspan can reach up to 8.2 feet? This symbolizes the expansive power we can access when we trust in God. While you are waiting, keep on worshiping and praying. Through worship and prayer, we can also renew our strength. Look to God, not people, for your strength. Human support is helpful, but ultimate strength comes from the Lord.

You will also, at times, have to speak to your soul. Engage in positive affirmations to remind yourself of God's promises. Like David in Psalm 42:5, declare, "Why are you cast down, O my soul? And why are you disquieted within me? Hope in God!" Fellowship is vital. Matthew 18:20 states, "For where two or three are gathered together in My name, I am there in the midst of them." Engage with those who uplift and encourage you in your faith journey.

Silence distractions in your life and find a quiet space to reflect and listen for God's voice. I love to ride my lawn mower or work in my yard. I even find peace in washing my cars. I usually listen to a sermon, a devotional, or worship music. Consider the Word as your portable charger. Whether through physical pages or an app on your phone, immerse yourself in Scripture. It's life-giving and essential for spiritual renewal. Serving can recharge your spirit by giving your time to others. Focusing on others helps you feel better and gets you out of your low point. Being active in service can bring a renewed sense of purpose.

Personal Reflection

1. Assess Your Spiritual Battery: Evaluate where you are spiritually. Are you feeling drained or energized? Identify areas needing attention.

   _____

   _____

2. Set a Prayer Schedule: Commit to daily prayer. Open your mouth and talk to God, asking Him to recharge your spirit.

3. Fellowship: Find a small group or friend who can pray with you and encourage you in your faith journey.

Conclusion

Reflecting on why my battery died, I realized it wasn't just a one- time incident; it was a lack of maintenance. Regular check-ups and addressing signs of wear early could have prevented that situation. Spiritually, it's the same. We must be aware of our spiritual battery—its condition and maintenance.

PRAYER

Dear Lord, Thank You for being my source of strength and renewal. Help me to recognize when my spirit is low and guide me to the actions that will recharge me. Teach me to wait upon You and to seek a community that uplifts and encourages. May I always find my strength in You, and may I never forget to maintain the battery of my soul. In Jesus' name, I pray. Amen.

DAY 5:

NO MATTER WHAT IT LOOKS LIKE

Scripture: Exodus 1:9-20

"And he said to his people, "Look, the people of the children of Israel are more and mightier than we; 10 come, let us deal shrewdly with them, lest they multiply, and it happen, in the event of war, that they also join our enemies and fight against us, and so go up out of the land."

Introduction

There's a story about a rich man's son who was a talented painter. One day, he decided to create a masterpiece. After days of hard work, he presented his painting to his father, but instead of admiration, he received criticism. The son felt disheartened, but continued to paint, pouring his heart into each stroke, regardless of the feedback. Eventually, the painting became famous, proving that sometimes, the world doesn't see the value of our work until much later.

Who Are You?

In the book of Exodus, we see a similar story unfolding with the Israelites. After Joseph and his generation passed away, the children of Israel multiplied and thrived. They were fruitful and enjoyed their lives, filled with love and hard work. But fear gripped the heart of a new king in Egypt, who saw their growth as a threat. To keep them in check, he placed taskmasters over them, aiming to suppress their strength.

The Israelites seemed to forget who they were—the descendants of Abraham, Isaac, and Jacob. The king's fear led him to impose harsh conditions on them. Yet, despite their oppression, the Israelites thrived. They had a resilient spirit, and in their struggles, they could still declare, "There is more for us than against us." When the enemy comes to afflict us, we must remind ourselves of our identity in Christ.

Pharaoh's decree to kill all male children was a dire threat. The midwives were caught in a perilous position, facing death if they disobeyed the king's command. Yet, they feared God more than they feared Pharaoh. This decision illustrates a profound faith and an understanding of God's authority. They recognized that their God was greater than any earthly power, and their courageous defiance saved many lives.

In Exodus 3:14, God reveals Himself to Moses as "I AM WHO I AM." This statement is powerful and reassuring. God is not limited by circumstances or appearances. He is the eternal, unchanging force who is always at work on our behalf. When we feel overwhelmed, we can hold onto the truth that "I AM" is with us.

Personal Reflection

1. Acknowledge Your Identity: Like the Israelites, remember who you are in Christ. Reflect on your heritage and the promises God has made to you. You are part of a larger story that transcends your current circumstances.

   _____

   _____

2. Fear God, Not People: In challenging situations, choose to fear God above all else. The midwives' bravery serves as a reminder that God's approval is far more significant than any human authority.

3. Declare the Truth: Speak life into your situation. When faced with obstacles, remind yourself and others that there is more for you than against you. Embrace the truth that God is always at work, even when you can't see it.

4. Trust in the "I AM": Whatever challenges you face, declare that God is "I AM." Trust that He is actively involved in your life, working behind the scenes for your good.

5. Look for God's Hand: In times of uncertainty, seek to recognize where God is moving. Even in the midst of adversity, He is crafting a plan for you.

Conclusion

The story of the rich man's son teaches us perseverance and the importance of believing in our work, despite others' opinions. Similarly, the Israelites and the midwives in Exodus exemplify unwavering faith in God's promises.

No matter what your situation looks like today, remember: I AM is working on your behalf. Embrace your identity, fear God, declare truth, and trust in His perfect plan. Your story is still being written, and the best is yet to come.

PRAYER

Heavenly Father, thank You for being "I AM" in my life. Help me to trust in Your plans, even when circumstances seem dire. May I find courage in my identity as Your child and boldly proclaim Your goodness. In Jesus' name, Amen.

DAY 6:

WORTH IT (DISCOVERING YOUR TRUE VALUE IN CHRIST)

Scripture: John 3:16

"For God so loved the world that He gave His only begotten Son, that whoever believes in Him should not perish but have everlasting life."

Introduction

We serve an awesome God who knows everything about us. He knows our names, our thoughts, our tears, and hears us when we call. He is a God who sees us, hears us, and knows us intimately.

For many of us, accepting this truth can be challenging. We often view ourselves through a distorted lens, shaped by our experiences, insecurities, and the expectations of others. Yet, the truth of John 3:16 reminds us of our worth in God's eyes: *"For God so loved the world that He gave His only begotten Son, that whoever believes in Him should not perish but have everlasting life."*

Our Worthiness

This verse is more than words; it's a profound declaration of God's love for humanity. It tells us that we are loved and valued beyond measure. God's love is not conditional. It's not based on our achievements, our past, or even our faithfulness. He loves us simply because He created us and desires a relationship with us.

Imagine the depth of love required to sacrifice your only child for people who are flawed and imperfect. Yet, this is what God did for us. He looked at each of us—our strengths, our weaknesses, our sins, and our potential—and decided we were worth the life of His Son. This realization should transform how we view ourselves and how we live our lives.

Let's be honest: We all struggle with feelings of unworthiness. Whether it's due to past mistakes, failures, or simply not feeling "good enough," these feelings can be crippling. I know this struggle well. Growing up, I battled with low self-esteem and a constant need to fit in. I compared myself to others, seeking validation in all the wrong places, and questioned my value and purpose.

But God doesn't see us the way the world sees us. He sees us as His beloved children. The Bible is filled with stories of people who felt unworthy or inadequate, yet God used them in mighty ways. Moses thought he was unfit to lead due to his speech impediment, but God called him to free the Israelites. Gideon saw himself as the least in his family, but God called him a "mighty man of valor" and used him to deliver Israel. David was just a shepherd boy, but God anointed him to be a king and a man after His own heart.

These stories remind us that God's view of us is not limited by our flaws or failures. He sees our potential, our hearts, and our willingness to be used by Him. When we begin to see ourselves as God sees us, it changes everything. When we look at John 3:16 through the lens of our personal struggles, we see a God who is not distant or indifferent. We see a God who is intimately involved in our lives, who understands our pain, and who values us enough to offer His Son as a sacrifice. This truth should shape how we see ourselves and how we live our lives.

In a world obsessed with perfection and comparison, it's easy to feel like we don't measure up. Social media, magazines, and even our peers set standards that are often unrealistic and unattainable. We end up chasing an ideal version of ourselves, thinking that if we can just achieve it, we'll finally be worth something.

But God didn't send His Son to die for the "perfect" version of you. He died for the real you—the you that struggles, the you that fails, the you that doubts. He saw your worth even when you couldn't see it yourself.

Instead of striving to fit in or meet the expectations of others, God calls us to embrace our identity in Him. In Jeremiah 1:5, God says, *"Before I formed you in the womb, I knew you; before you were born, I set you apart."* This verse tells us that we were created with a purpose and a plan. God knew every detail about us before we took our first breath, and He chose us to be His own.

Knowing this should free us from the burden of comparison and striving. You don't have to fit into someone else's mold because God created you to be uniquely you. Your gifts, your personality, your story—all of it is part of His design.

When you truly grasp how much God loves you, it changes everything. Instead of living for love, you begin to live from love. You no longer strive for acceptance because you know you are already accepted. You stop chasing after things that can never satisfy you because you've found your satisfaction in Him.

This is the freedom that comes from knowing your worth in Christ. It's not about what you've done or what you can do; it's about what He has done for you. It's not about earning His love; it's about receiving it and letting it transform you from the inside out.

Personal Reflection

1. Take a moment to reflect on how you see yourself. What lies have you believed about your worth?

   _____

   _____

2. Find a truth in Scripture that contradicts each lie. For example, if you've believed, "I am not enough," write down 2 Corinthians 12:9: *"My grace is sufficient for you, for My power is made perfect in weakness."*

   _____

   _____

Conclusion

Remember, your worth is not determined by your achievements, your past, or what others think of you. It is determined by the One who created you and gave His life for you. You are fearfully and wonderfully made, and nothing can separate you from the love of God. Embrace this truth and let it shape every area of your life. You are worth it!

PRAYER

Lord, thank You for loving me unconditionally. Thank You for seeing my worth even when I can't. Help me to let go of the lies and comparisons that hold me back. Teach me to see myself as You see me. Strengthen me in the areas where I feel weak and guide me as I walk in the path You've set before me. In Jesus' name, Amen.

DAY 7:

FAKE IT 'TIL YOU MAKE IT

Scripture: Isaiah 42:1-9

"Here is my servant, whom I uphold, my chosen one in whom I delight; I will put my Spirit on him, and he will bring justice to the nations."

Introduction

Have you ever found yourself merely going through the motions, or overwhelmed by your circumstances of life? Let's explore the concept of perseverance through faith, even when we feel we have nothing left to give. Learn the power of trusting God and continuing forward, believing that His strength is made perfect in our weakness.

Going Through the Motions

December 4, 1995 is a date I will never forget. It was the day that I lost my father, whom I resembled as my twin, and my best friend. My world seemed to quickly stop. Not to sound like a martyr, but my mother just lost her husband of twenty-six years, and my siblings also lost their father. My grandmother was suffering the loss of her son. However, there were things that had to be done.

I quickly took on the role of contacting extended family and friends, alerting them of this tragedy that was unlike anything my family had ever been through before. We did not have any experience in dealing with death, let alone how to plan a funeral service. I remember calling a family friend who used to help my parents with financial investments. We sat together at the dining room table in my parents' home sorting through any paperwork that resembled insurance, financials, and anything of significance. He guided me through the steps that needed to be taken. I also remember receiving recommendations for funeral homes. As I accompanied my mother to a meeting at the funeral home, I had an out of body experience. I did not recognize the woman walking into the funeral home. Surely it was myself, but I felt as though I was floating and it was all a dream.

Sitting in this cold building filled with death and sorrow, we began the process of planning my father's funeral. We answered and responded to questions that no child should ever experience. We toured a room full of caskets as if it were a car dealership. I certainly would have rather been selecting a new car than making my dad's funeral arrangements. We were tasked to answer questions about the obituary, photos, family, even the order of service for the funeral. Dealing with loss and the struggle of maintaining daily routines amidst grief was debilitating. Whether it's managing responsibilities after a loved one's death or simply facing the monotony of daily tasks, we sometimes feel like we are just "going through the motions." Somewhere in this process, God was giving us the strength to get through it all.

Personal Reflection

The familiarity of routines can feel like a burden, but they also provide stability during tough times. While routines might seem monotonous, it can also be a source of strength and discipline, such as maintaining a workout streak or a long-term marriage. You wake up, feed and dress the kids, and make it through the days just to start all over again. You may be a student or employee who wakes up to go to school or work to deal with the same people, same assignments, with little reward. Or, you find yourself in the cycle of having the same conversations with your loved ones or friends, over and over again.

Consistency, even in times of struggle, can yield unexpected benefits. The routine of a workout or the commitment to a marriage can bring physical, emotional, and spiritual rewards. Louis and I have been married over thirty years. OVER THIRTY YEARS. Let that sink in. There were periods of times when we were just going through the motions with the same old routine. Although we had periods of trials and tribulations, there are a lot of benefits to being married to him. The benefits of companionship, unconditional love, and intimacy. As far as my workout routine, I just wish that while I am exercising, God will also show up and ride my bike or walk on my treadmill for me! The routine and commitment to my workout routine isn't easy, and oftentimes, I am a zombie going through the routine; however, there have been remarkable benefits to sticking to it. It's not always about feeling enthusiastic, but about showing up and trusting that God will do the rest.

As Christians, we often struggle with giving 100 percent of our time, energy, dedication, and focus on God. When it doesn't happen, we internalize it as not being fit for the kingdom. The world teaches us that we have to give 100 percent to make it, and to simply believe in ourselves. When we don't measure up, we begin to internalize it as not being good enough for God's love. Just as we might struggle to give our best in relationships or personal goals, the same applies to our spiritual journey. We often feel inadequate, but God's grace is sufficient. *"But he said to me, 'My grace is sufficient for you, for my power is made perfect in weakness'"* (2 Corinthians 12:9). God invites us to bring our burdens to Him. It's not about giving 100 percent every day, but offering what we can and trusting Him to make up the difference.

God's Assignment

God's calling often pushes us beyond our comfort zone. He doesn't call us because we are ready or fully equipped, but because He has a purpose for our lives. "Fake it 'til you make it" means walking in faith, even when we feel unprepared. It means that even when you don't think you should be in the room, be in the relationship, get the promotion, God has a plan for your life.

"And we know that in all things God works for the good of those who love him, who have been called according to his purpose" (Romans 8:28).

Faith in Community

God often uses the people around us to support and encourage us. Whether it's a friend's timely text, a prayer from a loved one, or a simple act of kindness, these are reminders that we are not alone. *"Therefore encourage one another and build each other up, just as in fact you are doing"* (1 Thessalonians 5:11). If you don't have this type of support system, start building one. Pray and ask God to surround you with those who will support you and help you along your faith journey. *"Carry each other's burdens, and in this way you will fulfill the law of Christ"* (Galatians 6:2).

Personal Reflection

1. Reflect on times when you've felt like you were "faking it" in your faith or life.

   _____

   _____

2. What did you learn from those experiences?

   _____

   _____

3. How did God use those moments to strengthen you?

   _____

   _____

4. Did you ever get to a point where you felt like you made it?

_____

_____

PRAYER

Lord, cleanse the atmosphere around me. I am blessed, highly favored, fearless, and anointed. I am a child of the Most High God, created in Your image. Help me to trust in Your strength, especially when I feel weak. Help me to know that I am your servant and you personally called me! Amen.

DAY 8:

TRUST HIM

Scripture: Proverbs 3:5-6

"Trust in the Lord with all your heart and lean not on your own understanding; in all your ways submit to him, and he will make your paths straight."

Introduction

Trusting God can be one of the most challenging yet rewarding experiences of our faith journey. We often say we trust Him, but do we fully grasp what that means? Proverbs 3:5-6 urges us to trust the Lord wholeheartedly, without relying on our limited understanding. This kind of trust requires surrender and faith beyond what we can see or comprehend.

Unwavering Trust

Let me share a personal story about my journey of learning to trust God. There was a time when I thought I knew Jesus—I went to church, prayed occasionally, and believed in Him. But when life threw challenges my way I couldn't fix, I realized my knowledge of Jesus was superficial. I knew *of* Him, but I didn't *know* Him.

One day, I reached a breaking point. My plans were falling apart, and I felt like I was sinking. It was then that I decided to truly surrender to Him. I let go of my own understanding and asked Jesus to take control. At that moment, I can't really explain it, but I felt a peace and assurance like never before. I wasn't just believing in Him; I was *falling for Him*. And once you fall for Jesus, it's hard to imagine life without Him.

It is so freeing to know that we have a Savior who cares for us. When you come to a problem that you can't solve, it is so empowering to say, "Okay, God, this is now your problem." How are you going to solve this one? That is so freeing, knowing that he will see us through it. Trusting God didn't come to me overnight. It was through building a strong relationship with him that I truly began to trust him. It was through reading the Bible, praying, surrounding myself with other believers, and praise and worship that I developed this trust.

Let's look at some biblical examples of those who trusted God, even in the most daunting circumstances:

1. The Three Hebrew Boys (Shadrach, Meshach, and Abednego): They refused to deny God, even when threatened with a fiery furnace. Their trust wasn't contingent on being saved; they trusted God *regardless* of the outcome.

2. Daniel in the Lion's Den: He prayed faithfully, knowing his devotion to God could cost him his life. His trust was in God's sovereignty, not in his own safety.

3. The Woman with the Issue of Blood: She believed that if she could just touch the hem of Jesus' garment, she would be healed. Her trust in His power surpassed her fear of the crowd.

4. Noah: He built the ark for years, enduring ridicule, because he trusted in God's command and promise.

5. Paul: Despite persecution and hardships, Paul pressed on, shaking off every obstacle. His trust in Jesus kept him going.

6. Peter: Though he denied Jesus three times, Peter repented and went on to serve God boldly. Even when we falter, God is faithful in restoring us when we trust in Him.

7. The Shunammite Woman: When her son died, she declared,

8. "It is well," because she trusted that God had the final say.

Personal Reflection

1. Which of these stories resonates with you? How can their examples inspire you to deepen your trust in God?

   _____

   _____

2. Identify one area of your life where you struggle to trust God. Write a prayer of surrender, asking Him to take control.

   _____

   _____

Conclusion

Trusting God means surrendering every part of our lives to Him—our plans, our fears, our relationships, and even our disappointments. It's not always easy, but it's the only way to experience true peace and purpose.

PRAYER

Dear Jesus, I want to trust You more. Help me to surrender my fears and doubts to You. I know that Your plans for me are good, even when I can't see the way forward. Increase my faith and draw me closer to You. In Your name, I pray. Amen.

DAY 9:

DON'T JUDGE TOO QUICKLY

Scripture: Luke 10:25-26

"And behold, a certain lawyer stood up and tested Him, saying, 'Teacher, what shall I do to inherit eternal life?' 26 He said to him, 'What is written in the law? What is your reading of it?' 27 So he answered and said, 'You shall love the Lord your God with all your heart, with all your soul, with all your strength, and with all your mind,' and 'your neighbor as yourself.'"

Introduction

When I read the Word of God, I always seek to see how it relates to my life. The parable of the Good Samaritan brings to mind not just the characters in the story, but also our responses to others in need. As I read about the man who fell among thieves, I immediately thought of the thief mentioned in John 10:10: "The thief comes only to steal, and to kill, and to destroy. I have come that they may have life, and have it more abundantly."

Showing Mercy

A lawyer tests Jesus by asking, "What must I do to inherit eternal life?" Jesus responds by asking what the Law says, and the man answers: "Love the Lord your God with all your heart, soul, strength, and mind, and love your neighbor as yourself." Jesus affirms this, but the man, seeking to justify himself asks, "Who is my neighbor?"

Jesus then tells the parable of the Samaritan. A man is attacked by robbers, beaten, and left for dead. A priest and a Levite both pass by without helping. But a Samaritan—someone considered an enemy of the Jews—stops, cares for the wounded man, and ensures he receives further help. Jesus then asks, "Who was a neighbor to the man?" The lawyer replies, "The one who showed him mercy." Jesus tells him, "Go and do likewise."

Can you relate? In this story, which character resonates with you?

1. The Priest – the holy man of God.
2. The Levite – from the tribe of Levi, known for their service in worship and temple duties.
3. The Man on the Side of the Road – the one in need, perhaps the one who feels forgotten.
4. The Good Samaritan – the person who works behind the scenes, reaching out to help.

No matter how many times I read this parable, I find that God reveals new insights. Initially, I judged the priest and the Levite harshly. Questions filled my mind:

- Where were they coming from?
- How could they walk by and even cross to the other side?
- Were they good people or bad?
- Did they know the man? Perhaps they thought, *oh that's just so-and-so.*

We often make judgments based on appearances or past experiences. For all we know, they could have been praying for the man as they walked by, caught in their own struggles or simply thought it could be a trap to rob them.

Then there's the Good Samaritan, who took compassion on the wounded man. They saw someone who was in need and helped. They didn't think twice or wondered if this was a trap. He bandaged his wounds, pouring oil and wine on them, and took him to an inn for care. This story reminds me of Jesus:

1. He gets down on His knees to clean us up.
2. He pours in the oil and wine of healing.
3. He leads us to a place of refuge and comfort.
4. Though He must leave to prepare a place for us, He sends us a Comforter to ensure we are whole.

The Samaritan embodies the spirit of compassion and service, as Jesus. Where do you find yourself in life? Are you the one serving, the one in need, or somewhere in between? Are you leaving Jerusalem, the city of peace, heading toward Jericho, a city of destruction? Or are you on a journey from destruction towards the peace of God?

For all you Samaritans out there, remember not everyone is your assignment. When God wants to reach someone, He can use whoever is willing to be used, even those you least expect.

1. If the priest had stopped, he might have thought it was his duty.
2. If the Levite had helped, he might have felt the same obligation.
3. But when an enemy stops to help, it hits differently.

This is the heart of the Gospel. We have an obligation to spread the Word and act in love, regardless of our assumptions about others.

Personal Reflection

In what ways might God be calling you to step outside your comfort zone to serve others?

1. Evaluate Your Position: Are you too caught up in your own life to notice those in need around you?

    _____

    _____

2. Be a Good Samaritan: In what opportunities do you look to help others, especially those who may not be like you?

    _____

    _____

3. Avoid Quick Judgments: Remember, everyone has a story, and your compassion can bridge the gap. What ways can you be a gap changer?

    _____

    _____

Conclusion

Jesus described that when we help those in need, we're actually helping Him. When we see someone struggling, we're encountering a brother or sister of Jesus. Wouldn't we help Jesus' family? So, as you go about your day, ask yourself: Which one are you? And remember, don't judge too quickly. Let's strive to embody the love and compassion of the Good Samaritan, making a difference in the lives of those around us.

PRAYER

As I navigate life, please let me be mindful not to be so quick to judge someone. God, you are the true Judge and only you have that right to judge someone. In the future, let me be a blessing to someone else.

DAY 10:

HOW DO YOU SEE GOD?

Scripture: Matthew 16:15

"But what about you?" he asked. "Who do you say I am?"

Introduction

How we see God shapes how we live. If we see Him as distant, we may struggle to trust Him. If we see Him as loving and personal, we are more likely to rely on His guidance. Jesus asked His disciples, "Who do you say I am?" Their answer reflected their faith and understanding of Him. How would you answer that question today?

Entitlement

We often allow our circumstances to dictate how we view God. When life is good, we see Him as our provider and protector. But when trials come—when anxiety grips us, when prayers seem unanswered, when the future feels uncertain—we may question His presence and goodness.

Think about Peter. He saw Jesus perform miracles, yet in a storm, he doubted and sank. Moses saw God deliver Israel, but still hesitated at the Red Sea. Martha believed Jesus could heal, but when Lazarus died, she struggled to see His power beyond death.

Like them, we can have faith but still wrestle with doubt. Do we see God as powerful only when things go our way? Or do we trust that He is still working, even when we don't understand?

God invites us to see Him not just through our feelings, but through His promises. He is the same yesterday, today, and forever (Hebrews 13:8). He is our Shepherd, our Redeemer, our Peace. He sees our pain, our struggles, our needs—and He is faithful, even when we cannot see the full picture.

Personal Reflection

1. Reflect on Your View of God – Do you see Him as near or distant? Loving or harsh? Ask Him to reveal more of who He truly is.

   _____

   _____

2. Look for God in the Everyday – Keep a journal of moments where you see His presence, whether through people, nature, or unexpected blessings.

3. Strengthen Your Faith – Read stories in the Bible where God remained faithful, even in difficult times. Trust that He is still that same God today.

4. Declare Truth Over Your Doubts – When you feel afraid or uncertain, remind yourself of God's character. Say aloud: *God is with me. He is good. He will never leave me.*

Conclusion

How we see God shapes how we live, how we trust, and how we respond to life's challenges. If we see Him as distant, we may struggle with faith. If we see Him as harsh, we may live in fear. But when we see Him as a loving, present, and faithful Father, we walk in peace, trust, and confidence.

God reveals Himself in countless ways—through His Word, His creation, our experiences, and even in the quiet moments of our hearts. The question is not whether He is speaking, but whether we are willing to see Him for who He truly is.

Ask yourself today: How do I see God? And more importantly, am I willing to let Him transform my vision so I can see Him more clearly?

PRAYER

Father, help me to see You for who You truly are. Remove any false ideas I have about You, shaped by fear, doubt, or past experiences. Open my heart to trust You fully, even when I don't understand. Show me Your love, faithfulness, and presence in my daily life. I want to know You deeper and see You more clearly. In Jesus' name, Amen.

DAY 11:

THE GOD OF PEACE

Scripture: Philippians 4:1-9

*"Be anxious for nothing, but in everything by prayer and supplica-
tion, with thanksgiving, let your requests be made known to God; 7
and the peace of God, which surpasses all understanding, will guard
your hearts and minds through Christ Jesus."*

Introduction

As we approach the conclusion of Paul's letter to the Philippians, we
find him imparting crucial words of encouragement to a community
facing mounting challenges. The Roman Empire was tightening its grip
on Christians, escalating persecution and fear. Yet, amidst this turmoil,
Paul offers a message of hope, reminding us to stand firm in the Lord.

Rejoice in the Lord Always

Paul urges the Philippians not to sway in their faith, neither to the left
nor to the right. Our circumstances can easily dictate our emotional
and spiritual responses, but we are called to be steadfast. Jeremiah
17:7-8 paints a beautiful picture of what it means to trust in the Lord:
"Blessed is the man who trusts in the Lord, and whose hope is the

Lord." Like a tree planted by the waters, we can thrive even in the heat of trials.

We find Paul addresses a conflict between two women in the church. It's significant enough for him to call for unity and resolution. Division hinders our spiritual growth and effectiveness. A family that prays together truly stays together. When we disagree, we must learn to "agree to disagree" and maintain our focus on Christ. Unity is essential for us to prosper as God intends.

Rejoice in the Lord always. This joy comes not from our circumstances, but from our relationship with Him. By turning our eyes upon Jesus, we find a source of unshakeable joy. Prayer is the key to finding this joy. Prayer is our lifeline. Yet, many of us often turn to God only in times of need. Paul invites us to bring everything to God—our worries, desires, and thankfulness.

Take God out of the box and stop limiting His ability to show up. When we pray, we should approach Him with an open heart, inviting Him into every aspect of our lives. When we develop a relationship with God, He will give us a peace that surpasses all understanding. It's a peace that guards our hearts and minds, even amid chaos. This peace doesn't mean the absence of trouble, but rather a deep assurance in God's presence and sovereignty. When faced with overwhelming challenges—loss, financial strain, or relational turmoil—God's peace can sustain us.

Peter 5:8 warns us to be vigilant because our adversary seeks to devour us, often through our thoughts. Paul reminds us that our battles are spiritual, and we must equip ourselves with the armor of God to stand firm against the enemy's lies. When we neglect prayer and study the Word, we make ourselves vulnerable to doubt and fear. But when we truly meditate on whatever is true, noble, just, pure, lovely, and praiseworthy, these virtues transform our mindset and redirect our hearts towards God and His peace.

Personal Reflection

1. Spend a few moments each day in silence, reflecting on one of these qualities. Ask God to reveal how you can embody these traits in your life.

   _____

   _____

Conclusion

In Philippians 4:9, Paul assures us that if we practice what we've learned, the God of peace will be with us. When we focus on God, we gain the peace that surpasses all understanding.

PRAYER

Heavenly Father, thank You for being the God of peace. Help me to stand firm in my faith, seek unity with others, and rejoice in all circumstances. Teach me to pray with a heart of gratitude and to meditate on the truth of Your Word. Guard my thoughts and fill me with Your peace that surpasses all understanding. Amen.

DAY 12:

CLOSER IN SERVICE

Scripture: Ephesians 4:11-13

"And He Himself gave some to be apostles, some prophets, some evangelists, and some pastors and teachers, 12 for the equipping of the saints for the work of ministry, for the [a]edifying of the body of Christ, 13 till we all come to the unity of the faith and of the knowledge of the Son of God, to a perfect man, to the measure of the stature of the fullness of Christ."

Introduction

Jesus lived a life of service, demonstrating that true greatness comes not from being served, but from serving others. You are invited to reflect on your own journey as you begin to explore what it means to be closer in service to God and to one another.

In today's world, it's easy to fall into the trap of entitlement.

- What can you do for me?
- I want a job, but I don't want to work.
- I want things, but I don't want to pay for them.
- I want to be served, but not serve.

What's In It For Me?

These questions and thoughts can also creep into our spiritual lives. I remember a time when I felt that my mere presence should be enough. I thought, *They should be grateful I showed up*, and I wanted to hide in the back, selfishly contributing nothing. But the reality is, God has created each of us for a purpose, and there's always a way to serve. Ephesians 2:10 reminds us, "For we are God's workmanship, created in Christ Jesus to do good works, which God prepared in advance for us to do." We are all called to contribute; it's not just a few individuals who should bear the burden of ministry.

In 2 Timothy 1:9, we read, "It is God who saved us and chose us for His holy work." This powerful truth reminds us that we are part of one body, working together in unity. Every role is essential, and when we don't step up, we leave gaps in ministry. Just as in sports, where every player has a role, each of us has a part to fulfill in service to others. Consider how you might serve this week. Your actions can make a significant impact in your community and foster a sense of unity.

There is joy in serving. Galatians 1:15 states, "God, in His grace, chose me even before I was born and called me to serve Him." When we engage in our Father's business, we experience joy, peace, and the ability to bless others. Service takes our focus off our own issues and brings us closer to Jesus and to one another. Remember, the greatest service we can offer is to one another. 1 Peter 4:10 reminds us, "God has given each of you some special abilities; be sure to use them to help each other, passing on to others God's many kinds of blessings."

Personal Reflection:

As you reflect on your own life, think about the areas where you can serve. Here are some questions to guide you:

1. What gifts or talents has God given you? Identify how these can be used to bless others in your church or community.

   _____

   _____

2. What needs do you see around you? It could be something as simple as helping a neighbor with yard work or volunteering to organize church or civic events.

   _____

   _____

3. What is one step you can take this week? Commit to a specific action, whether it's signing up for a ministry, reaching out to a friend, or simply showing kindness to someone in need.

   _____

   _____

Conclusion:

To be closer in service is to be closer to God. As Martin Luther King Jr. said, "The time is always right to do what is right." He also posed a vital question: "What are you doing for others?" Remember, "Everybody can be great...because anybody can serve. You don't have to have a college degree to serve. You don't have to make your subject and verb agree to serve. You only need a heart full of grace. A soul generated by love."

PRAYER

Lord, help me to recognize the opportunities to serve within my community. Fill my heart with the desire to reach out to others, reflecting Your love through my actions. Help me to be mindful of the ways I can contribute to the body of Christ, serving with joy and purpose. Amen.

DAY 13:

BRING IT TO ME

John 4:13-14

"Jesus answered and said to her, 'Whoever drinks of this water will thirst again, 14 but whoever drinks of the water that I shall give him will never thirst. But the water that I shall give him will become in him a fountain of water springing up into everlasting life.'"

Introduction

When people think of being in ministry the first thing that comes to mind are facilitating seminars, formal evangelistic series, or other specialized ministries in order to properly spread the Gospel. I believe that true impact can also begin with one person at a time. The story of Jesus and the Samaritan woman at the well teaches us that sometimes we need to change our agenda to fulfill divine appointments, rather than our own.

Jesus was on a seventy-mile journey from Judea to Galilee and chose to pass through Samaria. This wasn't just a geographical decision; it was a purposeful one. The Bible says that he "needed" to go to Samaria. He even sent His disciples away so he could meet a woman at a specific well at noon. Jesus showed us that sometimes you have to change your agenda, route, and time just to meet that one person. This demonstrates that Jesus will go out of the way to have an encounter with you. He knew when to meet her, where to meet her, how to meet her, and what distractions needed to be removed. Here's the thing, this woman wasn't just any woman; she

was a Samaritan woman—an outcast in society. Jews despised Samaritans, yet Jesus broke societal norms just to engage with her. This had to be uncomfortable because a Jew and a Samaritan encounter was dangerous and forbidden. Not only did he meet her, Jesus engaged her in a conversation.

I can only imagine that while completing her daily chores, she wasn't expecting to see a man, especially a Jewish man. As the conversation unfolds, the woman is confused by Jesus' request for water. Yet, He offers her something far more valuable—living water. When Jesus tells her to bring her husband, He confronts her reality. She has had five husbands, and the man she is with now isn't her husband. The woman attempted to divert the conversation, but Jesus brought her back to the truth. He seeks those who worship in spirit and truth. Finally, Jesus revealed Himself as the Messiah. This is a pivotal moment not just for her, but for all of us.

I don't know where you are in your life right now, but Jesus is saying, *"I want to be with you."* You may think that you are a mess and can't get it right, but Jesus can handle it. If you are hungry, come and eat the bread of life. If you are thirsty, drink from the well that never runs dry. *"Come to me, all you who are weary and burdened, and I will give you rest. Take my yoke upon you and learn from me, for I am gentle and humble in heart, and you will find rest for your souls. For my yoke is easy and my burden is light"* (Matthew 11:28-30).

Personal Reflection

1. Jesus knows where to meet us, when to meet us, and how to meet us. Are you aware of how He orchestrates our encounters?

   _____

   _____

2. Jesus invites us to bring our burdens to Him. What do you need to lay down at His feet today?

   _____

   _____

3. As he did with the Samaritan woman, Jesus asks us to be honest about what holds us back. What sin/s or shame are you holding onto? Are you hiding behind a mask?

   _____

   _____

Conclusion

As we reflect on this encounter, let's pause and close our eyes. Imagine yourself at that well. Jesus is also there, inviting you to bring your burdens, your thirst for love, and your need for healing.

PRAYER

Lord, help me recognize my thirst and bring them to You. May I trust that You can satisfy my deepest needs. Let me be vessels of Your love, reaching out to those in need, one life at a time. Amen.

DAY 14:

FALLING FOR JESUS

Scripture: Matthew 14:29-31

"So He said, 'Come.' And when Peter had come down out of the boat, he walked on the water to go to Jesus. 30 But when he saw [a] that the wind was boisterous, he was afraid; and beginning to sink he cried out, saying, 'Lord, save me!' 31 And immediately Jesus stretched out His hand and caught him, and said to him, 'O you of little faith, why did you doubt?'"

Introduction

Have you ever experienced a moment when you felt completely out of control—when life seemed to be pulling you in a direction you never expected? Falling can be scary, whether it's physical, emotional, or spiritual. But what if falling wasn't about failure? What if it was about surrendering to the One who is always there to catch us?

Trust in Him

There was a time when I struggled with trusting God completely. I liked to be in control. I liked to plan, to know exactly how things would unfold, and to feel secure in my own understanding. But God had different plans.

Falling for Jesus doesn't mean losing. It means letting go of what we think we know and trusting Him to guide us. Life, much like faith, is not always about standing strong, but about knowing Who to lean on when we stumble.

Think about Peter walking on water. As long as he kept his eyes on Jesus, he did the impossible. But the moment he focused on the storm, he began to sink. Just like Peter, I have faced moments when I let fear, anxiety, and doubt distract me from my faith. But every time I've fallen, Jesus has been right there, extending His hand, ready to pull me back up.

God doesn't expect perfection from us. He doesn't love us less because we struggle. Instead, He uses our falling moments to draw us closer to Him. The beauty of falling for Jesus is that when we surrender our fears, insecurities, and doubts to Him, we discover that He is the safest place to land.

Personal Reflection

1. Examine Your Trust – Are there areas of your life where you are struggling to trust God? Write them down and pray over them, asking God to help you let go.

   _____

   _____

2. Look for Jesus in the Fall – When life doesn't go as planned, instead of resisting, ask God what He's trying to teach you through it.

3. Lean on His Word – Proverbs 3:5-6 reminds us that when we trust in God rather than our own understanding, He will direct our path. Memorize this verse and repeat it when doubt creeps in.

4. Surrender Daily – Each morning, start your day by saying, *"Lord, I trust You today. Even if I don't understand, I know You are guiding me."*

Conclusion

Falling for Jesus is not about losing control—it's about surrendering to the One who holds all things together. When we let go of our fears, our doubts, and our need for control, we fall into His grace, His love, and His perfect plan. Just as a child trusts their parents to catch them when they leap, we must trust that Jesus is always there, ready to uphold us with His unfailing love.

Life will present obstacles that make us hesitate, but when we choose to fall into His arms, we find strength, peace, and purpose beyond what we could imagine. So, let go of whatever is holding you back. Take that leap of faith, knowing that Jesus is waiting to catch you— every single time.

PRAYER

Heavenly Father, thank You for always being there to catch me when I fall. Help me to trust You with all my heart and to stop relying on my own understanding. When life feels uncertain, remind me that You are in control. Teach me to surrender to Your plans, knowing that You are leading me to something greater than I could ever imagine. Lord, I choose to fall into Your arms, knowing that I will always be safe in Your love. In Jesus' name, Amen.

DAY 15:

MAKE IT MAKE SENSE

Scripture: Mark 14:1-9

"While he was in Bethany, reclining at the table in the home of Simon the Leper, a woman came with an alabaster jar of very expensive perfume, made of pure nard. She broke the jar and poured the perfume on his head."

Introduction

The story of the woman with the alabaster jar is a powerful testament to love, sacrifice, and devotion. Her actions were misunderstood and judged by those around her, yet she focused solely on honoring Jesus. We invite you to reflect on our own acts of worship and the sacrifices we are willing to make for our faith.

A Sacrificial Love

When I read the New International Version of this story, there were a few words and phrases that stuck out for me. She was immediately ridiculed and judged for choosing this oil to use for Jesus. They questioned her choice of perfume and rebuked her harshly.

The story describes Jesus at the home of Simon the Leper in Bethany, just days before His crucifixion. The unnamed woman pours out an expensive perfume on Jesus, anointing Him in a powerful act of love and worship. Her actions were seen as wasteful by some, but Jesus honored her sacrifice. He recognized the depth of her love and the significance of her gesture, showing us that true worship comes from the heart. What a gentle spirit.

The alabaster jar of perfume was worth a year's wages, yet the woman did not hesitate to pour it out for Jesus. This act symbolizes giving our best to God, regardless of the cost. The disciples, particularly Judas, saw this as a waste, and, by the way, Judas betrays Jesus in the very next verse! But Jesus defended her, teaching us that the value of our worship is not measured by human standards, but by the heart's intention.

The woman's act of worship was criticized by those around her. This reaction is common even today, as people often judge others' expressions of faith. Whether it's the way someone prays, sings, or worships, we can easily fall into the trap of judgment. Jesus reminds us that worship is not about appearances, but about a heart devoted to Him. Our worship and praise is for Him.

Lessons from the Woman with the Alabaster Jar

The woman's story teaches us several valuable lessons:

- Worship Boldly: She wasn't afraid of what others would think. Her heart was set on honoring Jesus, no matter the cost. *"If anyone is ashamed of me and my words, the Son of Man will be ashamed of them when he comes in his glory"* (Luke 9:26).

- Give What You Have: She gave what she could, and Jesus commended her for it. God values the sincerity of our offering, no matter how small. *"Each of you should give what you have decided in your heart to give, not reluctantly or under compulsion, for God loves a cheerful giver"* (2 Corinthians 9:7).

- Your Worship Matters: Jesus said that wherever the Gospel is preached, her story would be told. Your acts of faith and worship have a lasting impact, even when they seem insignificant. *"Therefore, my dear brothers and sisters, stand firm. Let nothing move you. Always give yourselves fully to the work of the Lord, because you know that your labor in the Lord is not in vain"* (1 Corinthians 15:58).

Conclusion:

Her story is brief, but her impact is eternal.

The woman with the alabaster jar teaches us that worship isn't always neat, but it's often messy, emotional, and risky. She broke cultural expectations, poured out what was precious, and wasn't concerned about who was watching. Her act of worship was bold, vulnerable, and extravagant. She didn't come to impress—she came to surrender. Read that line again.

Jesus saw her. He heard the whispers, the judgment, the shame people tried to heap on her. But He called her action *beautiful.* While others saw waste, Jesus saw worship.

Here's a few reminders for the week:

- Don't let what others think keep you from pouring out your praise.
- Your past does not disqualify you from worship—God welcomes your broken pieces.
- What you bring to Jesus, no matter how costly, is never wasted.
- True worship is about the posture of your heart, not your perfection.

Personal Reflection:

1. What sacrifices have you made in your life as an act of love for Jesus? Have you ever felt judged for how you express your faith?

   _____

   _____

2. Is there something precious in your life that you are holding back from giving to God? What would it look like to surrender it fully to Him?

   _____

   _____

3. Have you ever judged someone else's way of worship? How can you change your perspective to honor God's work in their life?

   _____

   _____

4. What is one way you can worship God boldly this week?

   _____

   _____

PRAYER

Lord, help me to worship You boldly, without fear of judgment from others. Teach me to give what I have, trusting that You see my heart. May my life be a fragrant offering, like the woman with the alabaster jar, pouring out my love for You in everything I do. Amen.

DAY 16:

FINDING YOUR PEACE IN THE MIDST OF CHAOS

Scripture: Philippians 4:6-7

"Be anxious for nothing, but in everything by prayer and supplication, with thanksgiving, let your requests be made known to God; 7 and the peace of God, which surpasses all understanding, will guard your hearts and minds through Christ Jesus."

Introduction

In a world that often feels chaotic and overwhelming, finding peace can seem impossible. Yet, the Bible assures us that peace is available to us through Christ. Let's explore how we can access that peace, even in difficult times.

The Call to Prayer

Paul instructs us, "Do not be anxious about anything, but in every situation, by prayer and petition, with thanksgiving, present your requests to God." Prayer is our direct line to God. It is our most vital weapon in our arsenal that is rarely used. Oftentimes, we turn to professional help and medication before giving God an opportunity to support us.

There isn't anything wrong with these interventions, but He is also a support. How often do you turn to Him first when anxiety creeps in? In your own life, think about moments when prayer brought you peace. Paul continues to share in verse 7 this promise: "And the peace of God, which surpasses all understanding, will guard your hearts and minds through Christ

Jesus." This peace doesn't depend on our circumstances.

There is power in shifting our mindset from praying for ourselves versus incorporating thanksgiving into our prayers. When we acknowledge God's past faithfulness, we build a foundation of trust. This also provides us with a gentle reminder of the times when he was there for us in our time of need. 1 Thessalonians 5:16-18: "Rejoice always, pray continually, give thanks in all circumstances; for this is God's will for you in Christ Jesus." You may be reading this and thinking that this is easier said than done. I agree. It is.

Surely, I was not rejoicing and praying continually to God while our car was being repossessed. Nope. The first thing that went through my mind was how embarrassing this was, and how I was going to tell my wife. Once the initial shock and awe passed, I remember praying about it. I thanked God for the opportunity to have the vehicle in the first place. In the midst of our prayers and gratefulness, He reminded us that He is the God who restores. Several months later, my wife received an upgraded SUV, one of her dreams, but that is another testimony. "Set your minds on things that are above, not on things that are on earth" (Colossians 3:2).

Personal Reflection

1. Have you experienced a time when you felt inexplicable peace despite chaos?

   _____

   _____

2. Consider writing down three things you're thankful for each day. How does this practice change your perspective on your current challenges?

   _____

   _____

3. Our peace is often disrupted by the distractions of daily life. What are the "earthly things" that steal your focus from God?

   _____

   _____

4. Who are the people you surround yourself with that uplift and encourage you?

   _____

   _____

Conclusion

As we seek to find peace amidst chaos, let's remember that it is found in our relationship with Christ. He invites us to bring our worries to Him and promises to guard our hearts and minds.

> ### PRAYER
>
> *Lord, help me to cast my anxieties on You and to trust in Your peace that surpasses all understanding. May I seek You first in every situation and find rest in Your presence. Amen.*

DAY 17:

LEAN IN & PRESS ON

Scripture: Philippians 3:10-14

"...Forgetting what is behind and straining toward what is ahead, I press on toward the goal to win the prize for which God has called me heavenward in Christ Jesus."

Introduction

Have you ever felt stuck—trapped in anxiety, uncertainty, or fear of the unknown? You plan, you prepare, you do everything right, and yet, life still throws you into situations that feel impossible to navigate. You question whether you're on the right path. You wonder if God is really guiding you. Anxiety takes hold, whispering worst-case scenarios, making it difficult to move forward.

I've been there. I've battled the overwhelming fear of the unknown, the pressure of making the "right" decision, and the deep-seated worry that things won't work out. But Philippians 3 reminds us that we are called to press on, not because we have all the answers, but because we trust the One who does.

Just the Next Step

Although I did not know the name for it, anxiety has always been a struggle for me, and I've had moments where it has felt paralyzing. I remember when I lost my job unexpectedly. I had plans to grow and retire in this role as an educator. I invested ten years of my life building towards my career goals. My mind went into overdrive: *What will I do now? How will I pay my bills? What if I never find something better?* The uncertainty was suffocating, and I was overwhelmed by the thought of not being in control.

Then there was the time I felt God calling me to step into something new, something bigger than I had ever done before. Instead of excitement, I felt fear. *What if I failed? What if people judged me? What if I wasn't good enough?* The weight of those "what-ifs" almost kept me from stepping into the blessing that God had for me. But in both situations, God was teaching me something profound: *I don't have to have it all figured out to move forward. I just have to trust Him enough to take the next step.*

Paul understood this when he wrote to the Philippians. He acknowledged that he hadn't "arrived" yet, that his journey was still in progress. But instead of being stuck in the past or paralyzed by uncertainty, he made a decision: he would press on. He would move forward in faith, trusting that God had something greater ahead.

Anxiety tries to convince us that we need all the answers before we can take the next step. But God is calling us to walk by faith, not by sight (2 Corinthians 5:7). If we focus on our fears, we'll never move forward. But if we fix our eyes on Jesus and trust Him with each step, we will find the strength to press on, no matter what lies ahead.

Personal Reflection

1. Identify the fears that are holding you back. What is one area of your life where anxiety is keeping you from moving forward? Write it down and pray over it.

   _____

   _____

2. Replace fear with faith. Meditate on Philippians 3:10-14. Remind yourself that you don't need to have all the answers— God does.

_____

_____

3. Take the next step. You don't need to know the whole journey, but what is one step of faith you can take today?

_____

_____

4. Surround yourself with encouragement. Anxiety thrives in isolation, but faith grows in community. Find people who will remind you of God's promises and push you to keep moving forward.

_____

_____

Conclusion

Having faith and living in your faith are two separate things. You may believe in God, but sometimes not enough to step out. You can see the difficult thing ahead of you, but are afraid to take the next step. You are not alone. God is with you every step of the way. Once you take the initial step, you will run to the next!

PRAYER

Father, I come before You, laying my fears and anxieties at Your feet. I confess that I often try to control things that were never meant to be mine to control. Help me to trust You more. Remind me that You are guiding my steps, even when I can't see the full path. Give me the strength to move forward in faith, to press on, and to keep my eyes on You. I surrender my worries and place my trust in Your perfect plan. In Jesus' name, Amen.

DAY 18:

EVEN ME

Scripture: 2 Corinthians 12:9

"But he said to me, 'My grace is sufficient for you, for my power is made perfect in weakness.' Therefore, I will boast all the more gladly about my weaknesses, so that Christ's power may rest on me."

Introduction

Have you ever looked at your life and thought, *How could God ever use someone like me?* Maybe you've been overwhelmed by your past, your struggles, or the feeling that you are not enough. There was a time when I carried the weight of these thoughts. I questioned if I could truly be loved, if my mistakes and insecurities disqualified me from God's plan. But then, I encountered the life-changing truth of God's grace—it is for even me.

True Devotion

There are eight billion people on our planet and God created and knows each of us by name. His desire is for *each of us* to spend eternity with him, not eight billion minus one. He chases after the missing one until we are all back home with Him. I promise that if you feel that you are the lost one, you can be sure that He's searching for you right now and will never give up on you.

I always had a hard time relating my personal life to the lives of those in the Bible. I felt that their lives and situations were far away from me, and not real. However, throughout the Bible, we see God using the least expected people to accomplish His divine purpose. Moses was insecure about his ability to lead, yet God called him to deliver Israel. David made devastating mistakes, yet God still saw him as a man after His own heart. Rahab had a past, but her faith changed her legacy. Peter denied Jesus, yet he became the foundation of the early church. Paul persecuted Christians, but God transformed him into one of the greatest apostles.

At some point, we all struggle with the feeling of not being enough. I especially struggle when I compare myself to colleagues, or people who are doing things I always wanted to do. We think our failures, weaknesses, and insecurities disqualify us from God's love and purpose. But the reality is, our imperfections are the very places where God's grace shines the brightest.

I remember a season in my life when I felt completely unworthy. I was overwhelmed with anxiety, unsure of my purpose, and wrestling with feelings of doubt. My thoughts were loud: *You aren't strong enough. You don't have what it takes. You'll never be good enough.* But in that season, I learned a powerful truth: God's grace is greater than my self-doubt. His grace fills in the gaps where we fall short.

Personal Reflection

1. Stop disqualifying yourself. If God has called you, He has already factored in your weaknesses. You don't need to be "good enough"—you just need to be available.

_____

_____

2. Trade shame for grace. Your past does not define you. God's love is bigger than your mistakes. What shame do you need to trade for grace?

    _____

    _____

3. Say "yes" to God. Even if you feel unprepared, trust that God will equip you for the journey.

    _____

    _____

4. Encourage someone else. There are others struggling with the same feelings of unworthiness. Share your story and remind them that God's grace is for even them too.

    _____

    _____

Conclusion

Maybe you've been running from God, thinking you need to fix yourself before coming to Him. But the truth is, His grace is already waiting for you. God reminds us that His power is made perfect in our weakness.

PRAYER

Lord, thank You for Your grace that covers me, even when I feel unworthy. Thank You for loving me as I am and for calling me into something greater than myself. Help me to walk in confidence, knowing that I don't have to be perfect to be used by You. Teach me to embrace Your grace daily and to extend that same grace to others. I surrender my fears, doubts, and insecurities to You. Use me for Your glory. In Jesus' name, Amen.

DAY 19:

THE GOD OF SECOND CHANCES

Scripture: Micah 7:18

"Who is a God like you, pardoning iniquity and passing the transgression of the remnant of His heritage? He does not retain His anger forever, Because He delights in mercy."

Introduction

When I titled this *"God of Second Chances,"* you might have expected a typical devotional, and you'd be right—sort of. This is a message God placed in my heart, and I believe He wants to speak to you too. If I am real with you, I have struggled with my faith time and time again. If you've ever ridden a roller coaster, you know the highs and lows; that's how my faith journey has felt—like a never-ending ride.

My Second Chance

I remember when I lost my mother. I questioned God, feeling angry that He took her from me. I couldn't understand how he could take her from me at the age of fifty-four. She was too young to die. I wasn't ready or prepared when I got the phone call. I was in shock and paralyzed, not wanting to believe what I just heard. I cried out "Why, God?" I was angry and tempted to turn my back on Him.

I could hear the words of Job's wife: "Curse God and die." I had just lost my mother, the one whom I could call no matter what. I remember silently asking God "Why?" again. In the midst of my tears, He gently reminded me of a couple nights earlier. My mother was calling me, but I really didn't feel like talking. I wasn't busy. I wasn't doing anything. I just didn't feel like talking. Then a gentle voice said, "Pick up." Thank God I listened and picked up.

I picked up on the last ring. "Hello, Mom," I said. Our call didn't last five minutes. It was small talk and then she said, *"I just called to say, I love you."* I played those words repeatedly in my head. What I wouldn't give to talk to her again.

While I was questioning God again, He said I gave you those last moments. I whispered to answer the phone. He gently reminded me of my selfishness. My mother had been sick for some years, but nothing life threatening. But I had watched her quality of life decline over the years. I hated seeing my mom go through that phase. God's last question to me was "Do you want her to stay here and suffer?"

It is my prayer that one day I will get a second chance to see her in Heaven. Romans 8:28 assures us that all things work together for good for those who love God.

Have you ever questioned God? Have you asked yourself: Does God still answer prayers? Does He hear me and care about me? Why does He allow bad things to happen? Does He care about the desires of my heart?

Personal Reflection

1. Take a moment to reflect on your own life. Write down areas where you need to seek forgiveness or where you've been hesitant to accept God's grace.

   _____

   _____

2. What will you do differently moving forward?

   _____

   _____

3. Can you think of moments where God has given you a second chance? Remember, you are never beyond His reach.

   _____

   _____

Conclusion

Reflecting on life, I've fallen off the path more times than I can count and done things I hope are never discovered. There have been times I wanted to seek God yet felt no desire to do so, but His grace and mercy covered me. 2 Chronicles 7:14 tells us that if we humble ourselves, pray, and seek His face, He will hear us and heal our land.

It is God's desire that we all be saved. Because of His grace and mercy, He gives us chance after chance. Remember: it's not about how many times you fall, but how many times you get back up. We often say He is a God of a second chance, but in reality, He gives us countless opportunities to start anew. Every moment of your life is a second chance. Don't let the enemy's lies hold you captive.

PRAYER

Heavenly Father, Thank You for being a God of mercy and grace. I come before You, acknowledging my shortcomings and the times I've stumbled along my journey. I ask for Your forgiveness for my sins and for the moments I've doubted Your love and plans for my life. Help me to let go of the guilt and shame that I've carried. Thank you for giving me a second chance. In Jesus' name, I pray. Amen.

DAY 20:

LEAD INTO THE WILDERNESS

Scripture: Matthew 4:1-11

"Then Jesus was led by the Spirit into the Wilderness to be tempted by the devil."

Introduction

In the Gospel of Matthew, we encounter a pivotal moment in Jesus' life, one that follows His extraordinary baptism. It's fascinating how little we know about His life from age twelve to thirty, and yet the next major event after His baptism is him being led into the wilderness. One might expect a feast or a celebration after such a significant moment, but instead, Jesus is led by the Spirit into a desolate place, not for comfort, but for temptation.

The Wilderness Experience

Isn't it striking that we can be in the will of God and still find ourselves in a wilderness? The favor of God is real and beautiful, but it doesn't shield us from hardship. Often, when we find ourselves in difficult circumstances, we wonder, *How did I get here?* We might readily blame the devil for our trials, but sometimes, like Jesus, we are led there by God for a divine purpose.

The wilderness is a place of testing and preparation. Jesus had to confront His mission and prove His identity before beginning His ministry. This wilderness experience echoes the trials faced by Moses, who also struggled in a similar location, Mount Nebo, where he ultimately failed a critical test. Jesus' encounter with the devil in the wilderness serves as a powerful reminder of our own trials. The same wilderness where Moses wavered, Jesus must conquer. Each temptation offered by the devil is not just an attack, but a test of Jesus' resolve, faith, and understanding of His identity as the Son of God.

The First Temptation: Turning stones into bread (Matthew 4:3)—Here, the devil tempts Jesus to use His divine power to meet His own needs. Jesus responds, "Man shall not live by bread alone, but by every word that comes from the mouth of God." This reminds us that true sustenance comes from God's word, not merely from physical needs.

The Second Temptation: Testing God (Matthew 4:6)—The devil challenges Jesus to throw Himself from the temple, quoting Scripture to manipulate Him. Jesus counters, "You shall not put the Lord your God to the test." This teaches us the importance of discerning God's voice and not succumbing to temptation, even when it seems scriptural.

The Third Temptation: The offer of kingdoms (Matthew 4:9)—The devil offers Jesus all the kingdoms of the world, but how can one offer what belongs to someone else? Jesus knows He already holds all authority and power. His response, "Be gone, Satan!" illustrates the importance of recognizing our true identity and rejecting false offers.

In this wilderness journey, Jesus models how to combat temptation through Scripture and prayer. Each response He gives is rooted in His understanding of God's word. Coming face to face with the enemy, especially during our weakest moments, is not an easy feat. However, it's the perfect time to put to test the promises of God. The promises that He will never give us more than we can handle, or that He will never leave or forsake us. Try the Bread of Life for yourself so that when temptation arrives, you will be so full that the Word of God just rolls off your tongue.

Personal Reflection

1. Recognize Your Wilderness: Acknowledge when you're in a challenging season. Reflect on what God might be trying to teach you or prepare you for. Journaling your thoughts and feelings can help clarify your situation and lead you to discern God's purpose.

   _____

   _____

2. Turn to Scripture: Just as Jesus used Scripture to counter temptation, make it a habit to read and memorize passages that speak to your struggles. When facing challenges, recall these verses to strengthen your faith. Eat your bread and be filled.

   _____

   _____

3. Practice Prayer and Worship: Set aside dedicated time for prayer and worship. Use this time to pour your heart out to God, seek His guidance, and invite His presence into your wilderness. The wilderness can be a dark place without the Light of the world.

   _____

   _____

4. Surround Yourself with Support: Seek out friends or mentors who can pray with you and encourage you. Community can be a vital source of strength during tough times.

   _____

   _____

5. Embrace the Growth: Understand that wilderness experiences can lead to significant personal growth. Look for lessons in your trials and ask God to help you grow through them rather than just endure them.

Conclusion

As we navigate our own wilderness experiences, let's remember that God leads us with purpose. Each trial is an opportunity to strengthen our faith and clarify our calling. If God leads you to it, He will lead you through it. Every moment in the wilderness is preparing you for a greater destiny. Just as Jesus overcame temptation, so can we, by remembering who we are in Him and the power we have through His Word.

> ### PRAYER
>
> *Lord, thank You for leading me through the wilderness seasons of my life. Help me to trust in Your guidance and to stand firm against temptation. May I emerge stronger, with a clearer understanding of my purpose and identity in You. In Jesus' name, Amen.*

DAY 21:

"LOOK UP"

Scripture: Hebrews 6:9-12

"But, beloved, we are confident of better things concerning you, yes, things that accompany salvation, though we speak in this manner. 10 For God is not unjust to forget your work and [a] labor of love which you have shown toward His name, in that you have ministered to the saints, and do minister. 11 And we desire that each one of you show the same diligence to the full assurance of hope until the end, 12 that you do not become sluggish, but imitate those who through faith and patience inherit the promises."

Introduction

Life has a way of taking unexpected turns, often leading us to places we never imagined we'd be. I remember a particular moment in my life when I made a mess in my dad's car. He had given me some crackers to eat in the back seat of his car. At some point during our ride home, I fell asleep. When we got home, there were cracker crumbs all over his white leather seat. I was terrified because my dad kept a clean car. It was a small thing, but it felt monumental at the time. Just like that mess, life can throw us curveballs, leaving us feeling overwhelmed and lost.

My Journey of Faith

After graduating from college in August 2013, I had high hopes of landing a job right away. However, six long months passed with no prospects. During this time, I sought to help others, pouring my heart into ministry, even when my own situation felt bleak. I had to remember to praise God in the midst of my struggles.

Joseph's life exemplifies perseverance through adversity. His brothers, driven by jealousy, plotted against him, culminating in his being thrown into a pit. As I reflect on Joseph's journey, I can imagine the whirlwind of thoughts racing through his mind: What just happened? What did I do to deserve this? Why do they hate me so much? These questions resonate with many of us, especially young people facing betrayal or rejection.

In those moments of despair, a small voice whispers, *"Look up, I will never leave or forsake you. I won't give you more than you can bear. For I know the plans I have for you,"* declares the Lord, *"plans to prosper you and not to harm you, plans to give you hope and a future"* (Jeremiah 29:11).

I can almost hear Joseph in that pit, choosing to praise God despite his circumstances. His brothers might have wondered what was wrong with him, but Joseph knew he was a child of the King.

The Transformation of Trials

Joseph's story continues as he is sold into slavery, yet even in that situation, God was with him. Genesis 39:2-4 tells us that the Lord was with Joseph, and he prospered in everything he did. Even when he faced unjust imprisonment, he remained faithful.

- From Freedom to the Pit: Joseph went from freedom to a dark pit, a place of despair.
- From the Pit to Slavery: He was sold, but God's favor was still with him.

- From Slavery to Prison: Again, Joseph's faithfulness shone through.

- From Prison to Power: Ultimately, he rose to become second in command in Egypt.

Let's pause to take this all in. What a testimony for him to share with everyone! Joseph's journey reminds us that trials are often part of a greater plan. Each setback was a stepping stone leading to a significant purpose.

The Blessing of Forgiveness

When Joseph finally confronted his brothers, he chose mercy over revenge. This act of grace exemplifies the power of forgiveness. Just as God preserved Joseph, He may be preserving you through your trials.

Your blessings, like Joseph's tailor-made robe, are designed specifically for you. They might not come easily, but they are worth the wait.

Personal Reflection

1. Reflect on Your Trials: Take time to think about the "pits" you've found yourself in. What lessons can you learn from them? How can they shape your faith?

   _____

   _____

2. Embrace God's Promises: Keep scriptures like Jeremiah 29:11 close to your heart. Write them down and repeat them during tough times. They serve as reminders that God has a purpose for your life.

   _____

   _____

3. Shift Your Focus: Instead of dwelling on your circumstances, look up to God. Shift your attention from the problem to the One who holds the solution.

_____

_____

4. Practice Gratitude: Even in difficult situations, find something to be grateful for each day. This practice can transform your mindset and deepen your faith.

_____

_____

5. Trust the Process: Understand that God is working in the background, often in ways we cannot see. Trust that the blessings ahead are worth the trials.

_____

_____

Conclusion

If we put as much effort into serving God as we do into resisting Him, our lives would be transformed. God has a tailor-made robe just for you. Do you care? Do you want it? If you hold on and trust in God until the end, the blessings will always outweigh the costs.

Let us remember Joseph's story as we navigate our wilderness. May we learn to look up, praise God, and trust in His perfect plan.

PRAYER

Heavenly Father, thank You for the promise that You are always with me, even in my darkest moments. Help me to look up and trust in Your plan for my life. May I find strength in Your Word and grace in my trials. In Jesus' name, Amen.

DAY 22:

WHEN THE RIGHT THING IS THE RIGHT THING

Scripture: Daniel 3:26

"Then Nebuchadnezzar went near the [d]mouth of the burning fiery furnace and spoke, saying, 'Shadrach, Meshach, and Abed-Nego, servants of the Most High God, come out, and come here.' Then Shadrach, Meshach, and Abed-Nego came from the midst of the fire."

Introduction

Have you ever found yourself having to make a difficult decision? Do you stand for what is right, or do you stand with the majority? Often in life, I have found that the majority isn't always right. Following the latest trend or fad isn't the right thing to do. When you are standing for God or on His word, you sometimes find yourself on an island alone. It won't feel good, but it is the right thing to do.

Praise God

Think about the three Hebrew boys—Shadrach, Meshach, and Abed-nego. They stood firm in their faith, refusing to bow and worship the golden image despite the king's decree. They could have gone along with the majority, and no one would have said anything. But because they stood for God and on His word, they did the right thing. They refused to bow and were thrown into the fiery furnace that was turned up seven times hotter.

But when God is for you, He will protect you. No weapons formed against you will prosper. The same fire that was meant to kill them killed the men who were throwing them in. The same weapon the enemy was using was used against them. Because they stood alone and for what was right, God spared their lives. The fire only burned the very rope that was used to bind them.

When the king looked in, he saw not three but four people walking around in the fire. He even said that the four people looked like the son of God. King Nebuchadnezzar ordered them to be pulled out. What the enemy intended for evil, God turned it for His good. Nebuchadnezzar praised God. He made a decree that anyone who spoke against God would be punished and then he promoted Shadrach, Meshach, and Abednego to higher positions.

I've learned in life that people may criticize or mock your beliefs, but remember that their words don't define your worth. The world may try to constrain you with fear or societal pressures, but you have the power to break free through faith. They may even attempt to put you in situations meant to harm you. But in those moments, look closely—who is walking alongside you? Just like in the fiery furnace, God is right there with you, protecting you from the flames. You may emerge from trials unscathed, with no trace of what you've endured. Just as Paul declared, "Though He slay me, yet will I trust Him," we can find assurance in our trials. We serve a God who transforms what was intended for evil into good.

Personal Reflection

Reflect on your own trials and how God has walked with you through the fire. When faced with challenges, remember that you are never alone. Stand firm in your faith, knowing that God is transforming your struggles into testimonies of His goodness.

1. Identify Your Fires: What are the trials you're facing? Acknowledge them and bring them to God.

   _____

   _____

2. Remember Your Worth: Reaffirm that you are loved and valued by God. Speak truth over yourself daily.

   _____

   _____

3. Claim Your Inheritance: Take back what the enemy has tried to steal. Pray for restoration in your life.

   _____

   _____

4. Share Your Testimony: Let others know of God's faithfulness in your life. Your story could inspire someone else to stand firm.

   _____

   _____

Conclusion

As you stand for God and do what is right, remember that your faith can move mountains. God is with you in the fire, and you will emerge stronger, with a testimony that reflects His glory. Stand tall, knowing that you are worth it, and that your Savior lives!

PRAYER

Heavenly Father, I come before You with a grateful heart, acknowledging Your love and faithfulness in my life. Thank You for the examples of courage shown by the three Hebrew boys, Daniel, and the ultimate sacrifice of Your Son, Jesus. Lord, when I face trials and feel the heat of the fire, remind me that I am never alone. Help me to stand firm in my faith, even when the world tries to pull me away. In Jesus' name, I pray, Amen.

DAY 23:

THE DREAM KILLER

Scripture: Genesis 37:19-20

"Then they said to one another, 'Look, this dreamer is coming! Come therefore, let us now kill him and cast him into some pit; and we shall say some wild beast has devoured him. We shall see what will become of his dreams!'"

Introduction

Dreams are powerful. They inspire us, motivate us, and push us to become more than we ever thought possible. Yet, they can also lead us into the depths of despair when we face opposition. In Genesis 37, we encounter Joseph, a young man with a grand dream that ultimately lands him in a pit. As I reflect on my own dreams and the trials I've faced, I realize how easy it is to let discouragement dim the light of our aspirations. I am a dreamer.

Shaking it Off

As I look at my life, I think back to a time when I felt my own dreams slipping away. I had a vision for my career and life, but unexpected setbacks and harsh criticism from others left me questioning my worth and purpose. In those moments, I felt as if I were in my own pit, surrounded by darkness. But like Joseph, I learned that the pit isn't always a bad place.

Joseph's brothers were jealous of him, especially after he shared his dreams of greatness. Their response? They threw him into a pit, a place of despair and abandonment. When you find yourself in a pit—whether due to betrayal, disappointment, or failure—it can feel as though your dreams are buried beneath the weight of your circumstances.

But here's the truth: being in a pit doesn't mean your dreams are dead. It's a reminder that God can bring new life from even the most hopeless situations. I remember a time when I faced a significant setback. I could have let the disappointment crush my spirit, but instead, I chose to look for the lesson in the struggle.

In the pit, Joseph had two choices. He could succumb to self-pity and bitterness, or he could choose to praise God, trusting that He had a greater plan. Many of us find ourselves in similar situations. When faced with adversity, we can either wallow in despair or lift our hands in praise.

Imagine Joseph in that dark pit, wrestling with feelings of betrayal and fear. Yet, despite it all, he made the right choice. I encourage you to make the same choice. When life feels overwhelming, turn your focus toward gratitude and praise.

The story of the donkey that fell in the pit illustrates resilience beautifully. The owner saw that there was no way he could save the donkey so he decided to bury the donkey. When the owner started shoveling dirt into the pit, the donkey could have given up. Instead, it began to shake off the dirt and step up, realizing that each shovelful was a way to rise higher.

What dreams are you nurturing that feel buried under layers of disappointment? Use those struggles as fuel. Let them propel you upward rather than weigh you down. When I faced criticism and doubt, I used that energy to work harder and stay focused on my vision. Remember 2 Chronicles 20:15: "The battle is not yours, but the Lord's." Believing that God is fighting for you changes how you approach your challenges.

Personal Reflection

1. Write down three things you are grateful for right now. When you feel your dreams are threatened, revisit this list and remind yourself of God's goodness.

   _____

   _____

2. Share a moment when you turned adversity into motivation. How did that shape your journey?

   _____

   _____

Conclusion

The journey toward fulfilling our dreams may be fraught with challenges, but it's a journey worth taking. Remember that God is with you through every trial. He has a plan for your life, and the pit is just a temporary stop on the way to your destiny.

PRAYER

Heavenly Father, thank You for the dreams You've placed in my heart. Help me to trust You during the trials I face. May I rise above discouragement and keep my eyes fixed on You. Give me the strength to persevere and the wisdom to surround myself with those who uplift me. I believe that with Your help, I can achieve all that You have planned for my life. Amen.

DAY 24:

STANDING FIRM IN THE MIDST OF TRIALS

Scripture: Ephesians 6:13

"Therefore put on the full armor of God, so that when the day of evil comes, you may be able to stand your ground, and after you have done everything, to stand."

Introduction

Standing firm is often easier said than done. There are seasons in life when everything seems to conspire against you—your health, finances, relationships, and even your faith. You may find yourself knocked down repeatedly, wondering how you can possibly get up again. It's in these moments that standing isn't just about resilience; it's about faith and trust in a God who never leaves us or forsakes us. The Apostle Paul understood this struggle. Writing from prison, he encouraged the believers in Ephesus to stand firm in their faith, even amidst trials and persecution. His words still resonate today, calling us to take up the full armor of God and stand, no matter what life throws our way.

Learning to Stand

A few years ago, I faced one of the toughest seasons of my life. I felt like everything was falling apart. I was dealing with a difficult work situation and with deteriorating knees, and I felt isolated and alone. No matter how hard I prayed, the circumstances around me wouldn't change. I was exhausted—emotionally, physically, and spiritually.

One night, I found myself praying, tears streaming down my face. "God, I don't know how much more I can take," I whispered. In that moment of raw honesty, I felt God's presence surround me with a simple message: "Stand." It wasn't an answer to all my problems or a miraculous intervention, but it was the encouragement I needed. I wasn't called to fix everything or to carry all the burdens on my own. I was simply called to stand—in faith, in trust, and in hope.

But why is standing so important? Standing is an act of defiance against the enemy. It's saying, "I won't be moved by fear, doubt, or despair." It's declaring that God is your strength when you feel weak, your peace when you're surrounded by chaos, and your hope when everything seems hopeless. When we stand, we acknowledge that God is in control, even when our circumstances suggest otherwise. We trust that His plans for us are good, even when we don't understand them (Jeremiah 29:11).

The enemy's goal is to make us doubt God's goodness, His faithfulness, and His love for us. By standing firm, we protect our faith from being eroded by fear and uncertainty. When people see us standing firm in our faith, even during trials, it speaks volumes about the God we serve. Our endurance becomes a testimony of God's sustaining power and His ability to carry us through the storm.

Standing Strong in My Own Life

When I look back on the challenging seasons in my life, I see God's faithfulness woven through every moment. There were times I felt overwhelmed, defeated, and tempted to give up. But God's Word and the support of others helped me to stand firm. Standing firm is not just about holding your ground; it's about trusting God to be your strength and shield. When you've done all you can do, keep standing, because God is standing with you.

Standing When Your Health Fails: When I was dealing with the health of my knees, the pain of arthritis was so annoying. From aqua therapy, physical therapy, and medications, it was inevitable that I was going to require surgery. I remember the overwhelming fear and uncertainty that loomed over me like a dark cloud. I clung to verses like Isaiah 41:10, where God promises, *"So do not fear, for I am with you; do not be dismayed, for I am your God. I will strengthen you and help you; I will uphold you with my righteous right hand."* Every doctor's visit, every painful procedure, I whispered these words, asking God to be my strength.

Standing in the Face of Injustice: I have faced situations where I felt unheard and unseen because of my race and background. It was frustrating and disheartening, making me want to retreat and not engage with others. During these times, God reminded me of the power of standing in truth and love, even when it's uncomfortable. I learned to speak up, not in anger, but with grace, trusting that God would be my voice.

Standing When Relationships are Strained: There were moments when our marriage was strained, and reconciliation seemed impossible. We've been married over thirty years, so challenges are inevitable. After much deliberation and therapy, we chose to stand in prayer and love, even when it felt like I was standing alone. It wasn't easy, and it didn't always lead to immediate healing, but God worked on my heart, teaching me patience and perseverance. Surrounding ourselves with family and friends who pray and support us was paramount.

Personal Reflection

1. Start Each Day with Prayer: Before you face the day, take time to connect with God. Ask Him for strength, wisdom, and guidance. Surrender your day to Him and invite Him to go before you in every situation.

   _____

   _____

2. Stay Grounded in Scripture: Get to know Jesus for yourself, as your personal friend. Make it a habit to read and meditate on God's Word daily. The more you fill your mind with His truth, the less room there is for the enemy's lies.

   _____

   _____

3. Surround Yourself with Encouragement: Find or create a community of believers who will lift you up in prayer and encourage you in your walk with Christ. There's a difference in just being surrounded with people and noise, versus surrounding yourself with prayer warriors and supporters. We're not meant to stand alone; we need each other.

   _____

   _____

4. Remember God's Faithfulness: Reflect on past experiences where God has come through for you. Let those memories build your faith and remind you that if God was faithful then, He will be faithful now. I promise.

   _____

   _____

Conclusion

Trials will come, but they do not have the power to shake the foundation of our faith unless we allow them to. Standing firm does not mean we won't feel the weight of hardship—it means we choose to anchor ourselves in God's promises despite the storm. As James 1:12 reminds us, *"Blessed is the one who perseveres under trial because, having stood the test, that person will receive the crown of life that the Lord has promised to those who love him."*

When difficulties arise, let them push you closer to God, not away from Him. He is your strength, your refuge, and the One who sustains you. Hold fast to His Word, trust in His faithfulness, and stand firm—knowing that every trial is an opportunity for spiritual growth and a deeper relationship with Him.

PRAYER

Lord, thank You for equipping me with everything I need to stand firm in my faith. Help me to remember that I don't stand alone; You are with me, fighting my battles and strengthening me. When I feel weak, please remind me that Your strength is made perfect in my weakness. Help me to put on the full armor of God each day and to stand firm against the enemy's schemes. I trust You, Lord, and I surrender my fears and anxieties to You. In Jesus' name, Amen.

DAY 25:

ENCOUNTERING CHANGE IN HIS PRESENCE

Scripture: Luke 17:11-19

"Now it happened as He went to Jerusalem that He passed through the midst of Samaria and Galilee. 12 Then as He entered a certain village, there met Him ten men who were lepers, who stood afar off. 13 And they lifted up their voices and said, 'Jesus, Master, have mercy on us!'"

Introduction

Let's talk about the transformative power of worship. If there's one word that encapsulates our encounters with God each week, it's change. The question is when you leave the presence of God, have you been changed? Transformation and change can appear in many different forms. Some have experienced an immediate conviction, while others experience a longing to learn more about Him. There is no prescription for exactly how the change will occur, but trust that you will experience something powerful and different.

The Call for Change

Have you ever walked into a church or read a devotional message and thought, *This message must have been for someone else because I didn't get anything out of it?* Or maybe you've felt the temptation to drift off during a message or prayer? If we come seeking God, but focus on distractions, we miss the point. If you're not encountering Him, ask yourself why. Are you doing it out of routine, obligation, or to simply check it off your list?

If you genuinely seek Him, you will find Him. Don't judge your experience based on someone else's. The greatest tragedy is to be in the presence of God and leave unchanged. Truly worshiping God should transform us; being in His presence should bring about change. Just as you wouldn't accept a faulty repair on your car, why should we accept leaving God's house unchanged? Jeremiah 29:13 (NIV) says, "You will seek me and find me when you seek me with all your heart."

The Lesson from the Lepers

The Bible introduces us to ten lepers in Luke Chapter 17. They suffered from a disease that began with a small spot, leading to their ostracization. Over time, if left unchecked, it would spread and alter their lives drastically. Isn't this how sin operates? It starts small— a glance, a message—and, if not kept in check, can grow uncontrollably.

These men witnessed their bodies deteriorate and their lives change. Sin can create a similar decay in our relationships, turning laughter into silence. When burdened by sin, we often look to others to feel better about ourselves, but this only deepens our isolation.

The Good News of Jesus

In spite of their dire situation, one day, they encountered Jesus— someone who crossed societal boundaries to meet them. No matter where you are, Jesus meets you there. He sees your struggles, even when you try to hide them.

When the lepers recognized who was among them, they remembered all the miracles He had performed: the blind seeing, the lame walking, the dead being raised. They realized that with Jesus, change was not only possible; it was inevitable. At some point, you must be sick and tired of being sick and tired. If you're seeking a blessing today, don't leave his presence until you've experienced change.

Stepping Out in Faith

The lepers cried out, "Jesus, Master, have mercy on us!" (Luke 17:13). They acknowledged His power and their need for grace. Jesus instructed them to show themselves to the priests, even before they were healed. This act of faith was crucial. Hebrews 11:1 teaches us, "Now faith is the assurance of things hoped for, the conviction of things not seen." Faith opens the door for God to act. Act as if your healing is on the way. Thank Him in advance for what He will do. As they headed to the priest, something miraculous happened: they were healed on their way (Luke 17:14).

Personal Reflection

1. Describe the last time you felt the presence of God. Did you recognize it in the moment, or discover it later?

   _____

   _____

2. What changes are you trusting God for?

   _____

   _____

Conclusion

Among the ten, only one returned to thank Jesus (Luke 17:15-16). He was made whole—not just healed but restored. When we encounter

God's presence, let gratitude fill our hearts. Every time we are in His presence, we should expect change.

PRAYER

Lord, help me to be open to change in Your presence. Help me to leave trans-formed and ready to lead the changes I want to see, according to your will. Amen.

DAY 26:

FORGIVENESS

Scripture: 2 Corinthians 3:17

"Where the Spirit of the Lord is, there is freedom."

Introduction

Let's contemplate the magnitude of God's grace and the power of forgiveness. Imagine the Apostle Paul singing, "How great is our God?" on his road to Damascus. This man, once a persecutor of Christians, had a life-changing encounter with Jesus, transforming him into one of the most influential voices in the early church. Paul's story is a testament to what can happen when the Spirit of the Lord intervenes. If God could take someone like Paul and turn him into a beacon of hope, then truly, there is hope for me!

Forgive and Forget

When I lost my job, it forced me to reevaluate my identity and my reliance on worldly circumstances. My self-worth and identity were lost in my role and position. It was through this trial that I experienced the profound need for forgiveness and freedom. I needed to forgive those whom I thought did me wrong. I needed the freedom to be able to be at peace and sleep at night. The enemy seeks to imprison us in our sins, secrets, and lies. But God, in His infinite mercy, offers us life in abundance (John 10:10). Jesus declared, "The Spirit of the Lord is on me...to proclaim freedom for the prisoners" (Luke 4:18). There is a difference between the words forgive, forgiveness, and forgiven.

Forgive: To forgive is to stop feeling angry or resentful toward someone for an offense, flaw, or mistake. The word "forgive" appears forty-two times in the Old Testament and thirty-three times in the New Testament (NIV). We often say, "I forgive you, but I will never forget." But did we truly forgive? Imagine if God responded similarly: "I forgive you, but I won't forget." That's a notion planted by the enemy. True forgiveness leads to healing and release. Hebrews 8:12 assures us: "For I will forgive their iniquities, and I will remember their sins no more."

Forgiveness: Forgiveness is the action or process of forgiving or being forgiven. The word appears fourteen times in the Old Testament and thirteen in the New Testament. Psalm 130:3-4 reminds us: "If You, Lord, should mark iniquities, O Lord, who could stand? But there is forgiveness with You." Many of us have experienced the liberating power of forgiveness—what a sense of release and freedom! The adversary doesn't want us to know that freedom; he wants us to live in guilt.

Forgiven: To be forgiven means to grant pardon to someone. This term appears seventeen times in the Old Testament and twenty-eight times in the New Testament. Consider who God has forgiven: David, a murderer and an adulterer; Saul, a murderer of Christians; Jonah, who attempted to flee from God; and Jacob, a deceiver. If God can forgive these individuals, He can forgive us too.

Personal Reflection

1. I remember leading a class where I asked them to write down any unforgiveness or burdens on a piece of paper. I had them place it in a bowl of water, symbolizing the act of letting go. This helped me gain a sense of freedom, a peace of mind, or release. Micah 7:19 says, "You will again have compassion on us; you will tread our sins underfoot and hurl all our iniquities into the depths of the sea." Continue your understanding of forgiveness by reading Matthew 6:14-15, Mark 11:25 and 1 John 1:9.

   _____

   _____

Conclusion

We must also learn to forgive ourselves. The enemy desires to keep us bound in secrets, lies, and unforgiveness. Now is the perfect time to let go. When you are in Christ, you are not defined by your past sins or the labels the world places on you. You are forgiven, and the Holy Spirit dwells within you. Remember, "Where the Spirit of the Lord is, there is freedom."

PRAYER

Dear heavenly Father, please forgive me for not forgiving others and myself. Help me to live a life that is pleasing to you, and no matter who has offended me, let me have the spirit of forgiveness.

DAY 27:

HIS POWER WITHIN US

Scripture: Ephesians 3:14-21

"... I pray that out of his glorious riches he may strengthen you with power through his Spirit in your inner being, so that Christ may dwell in your hearts through faith. And I pray that you, being rooted and established in love, may have power, together with all the Lord's holy people... —that you may be filled to the measure of all the full-ness of God."

Introduction

I often think of my grandmother, a woman who was filled with pas-sion and love. Her energy was infectious, inspiring those around her. I admired her strength and unwavering faith, and it makes me reflect on my own journey with God. For a time, I treated my relationship with Him like a hobby—something I engaged in only when convenient. But when we allow our passion for God to flourish, receiving his Power, our entire lives transform.

Rise Up

Understanding who God is—this is essential for experiencing His power. He is not merely a distant deity; He is our Father, our friend, the one who sent His Son to die for us. He desires a deep relationship with us, one where His power can flow freely into our lives. Paul reminds us that this power strengthens us through His Spirit in our inner being, allowing Christ to dwell in our hearts. God wants us to experience His fullness both on earth and in heaven. He desires for us to live abundant lives filled with joy, peace, and purpose. Yet, we face an adversary who seeks to steal our happiness, joy, and peace. The enemy delights in our struggles and will attempt to knock us down.

Life can throw unexpected challenges at us: job loss, the death of a loved one, health diagnoses, or the end of relationships. These moments can leave us feeling defeated. Remember, the enemy is out to trip us up, but these setbacks do not define us. Acknowledge your situation. Allow yourself the space to grieve, to cry, and to reflect. This may feel uncomfortable, but it's a necessary step. In this time, friends can be a great support, just as Job had his friends who sat with him in silence. This step may last longer than we'd like, but it's part of the healing process.

After you've processed your feelings, it's time to rise up. Find your strength in God. Begin to praise Him, just as Job did, even in his suffering. Turn on worship music, read Scriptures that affirm your identity and promises from God. Engage in prayer and declare God's Word over your life. Start declaring Deuteronomy 28:13 over your life, I am the head and not the tail. I can do all things through Christ who strengthens me (Philippians 4:13). Weeping may endure for a night, but joy comes in the morning (Psalm 30:5). No weapons formed against me shall prosper (Isaiah 54:17).

Personal Reflection

1. Identify Your Struggles: Write down the areas where you feel knocked down. Take them to God in prayer.

   _____

   _____

2. Seek Community: Reach out to a trusted friend or a support group. Share your burdens and allow others to bear them with you.

   _____

   _____

3. Engage in Worship: Set aside time for worship, whether through music, prayer, or journaling. Let your heart connect with God's power.

   _____

   _____

4. Claim His Promises: Regularly meditate on Scripture. Write down verses that resonate with you and declare them daily. Personalize them by adding your name.

   _____

   _____

Conclusion

The power within us is not our own—it is the power of Christ working through us. When we surrender our weaknesses to Him, we find strength beyond our understanding. God has placed His Spirit in us, equipping us to overcome obstacles, face our fears, and step into His purpose with confidence.

No matter how unqualified or incapable we may feel, the truth remains: _"Greater is He that is in you than he that is in the world."_ (1 John 4:4)

Lean into that power. Trust that God's strength is made perfect in your weakness. Walk forward boldly, knowing that you are never alone, and that within you lies the power to do more than you could ever imagine—through Him.

PRAYER

Lord, Thank You for the power that resides within me through Your Holy Spirit. Help me to remember that I am never alone in my struggles. When I feel knocked down, remind me to turn to You for strength and comfort. Teach me to embrace the fullness of Your love and to live boldly in the promises of Your Word. As I navigate life's challenges, may I cling to You and recognize the power that You have placed within me. Let me rise up in faith, knowing that with You, I can overcome any obstacle. In Jesus' name, I pray. Amen.

DAY 28:

IN THE NAME OF JESUS

Scripture: Acts 3:1-10

"One day Peter and John were going up to the temple at the time of prayer—at three in the afternoon. Now a man who was lame from birth was being carried to the temple gate called Beautiful, where he was put every day to beg from those going into the temple courts..."

Introduction

In this powerful story, we see Peter and John going to the temple at the hour of prayer. They encounter a man who has been lame from birth, placed daily at the Beautiful gate to beg. This man's existence represents so many of us—relying on the kindness of others while being overlooked by society.

It is interesting that the man is brought to the gate, but not inside the city. It is like carrying him to the door of the church, but not inside. How many times have we come to the edge of a breakthrough and stopped right before we received our blessing? We see that this man was looking to get his monetary needs met. Many people ignored him and just kept on walking.

Peter and John were on their way to worship, and because of their commitment to consistent worship, they recognized the man's need. When you consistently worship, God will open your spiritual eyes to see the needs around you. It's not about looking for opportunities to minister; it's about being so immersed in worship that you naturally see and respond to those needs.

Walking with God

Their act of worship led them to a divine appointment. They didn't just ignore the man; instead, they were led to address his greater need—mobility instead of mere money. He asked for financial help, but God wanted to give him a life-changing miracle. Sometimes our prayers are too low. We need to elevate our expectations of what God can do. Acts 3:6-8 says, "Silver or gold I do not have, but what I do have I give you. In the name of Jesus Christ of Nazareth, walk." Taking him by the right hand, he helped him up, and instantly the man's feet and ankles became strong. He jumped to his feet and began to walk. Then he went with them into the temple courts, walking and jumping, and praising God.

Peter and John said, "In the name of Jesus Christ of Nazareth, walk!" They didn't rely on rituals or fancy prayers; they simply called upon the powerful name of Jesus. Names hold tremendous power. Neuroscience has shown that the words we speak can influence our physical and emotional health. Proverbs 18:21 tells us that the tongue holds the power of life and death. When you call on the name of Jesus, endorphins flood your system, enhancing your well-being.

There is undeniable power in the name of Jesus! It is the name that has the power to set the captive free, to make the lame walk, the blind to see, and to heal the sick. It mends the brokenhearted. My mother would often remind me, "Jesus will make a way out of no way." My father would encourage me, saying, "Just call on Him." My wife would often exclaim, "Won't He do it?" And I declare, He is my calm in the midst of the storm.

Personal Reflection

1. Describe the last time you tested and tried on the power of Jesus?

   _____

   _____

2. Are you comfortable with praying for or with others?

   _____

   _____

3. Ask God for the opportunity to see and respond to someone in need this week.

   _____

   _____

Conclusion

So, let me ask you, what name do you call upon in times of trouble? The name of Jesus can change your atmosphere. When my grandmother walked through her home calling on the name of Jesus, she understood the transformative power in that name.

Today, let's choose to call on that name. Let's be consistent in our worship and aware of the needs around us. When we do, we not only elevate our own lives, but also the lives of those around us. In the name of Jesus, there is healing, freedom, and transformation waiting to be unleashed. Amen.

PRAYER

Thank You for the power in the name of Jesus. Thank You for the miracles You perform in my life, both seen and unseen. Help me to be consistent in my worship and sensitive to the needs of those around me. Open my eyes to see the opportunities to serve and uplift others. May I always remember that, in Your name, there is healing, freedom, and hope. Empower me to be instruments of Your grace, sharing the good news with those in need. I ask this in the powerful name of Jesus. Amen.

DAY 29:

IT IS FINISHED

Scripture: John 19:30

"When Jesus had received the sour wine, he said, 'It is finished,' and he bowed his head and gave up his spirit."

Introduction

Have you ever experienced the weight of debt? That sinking feeling that comes when obligations press down on you, making every breath a little heavier? As we reflect on the cross, we see a different kind of debt being paid. Jesus went willingly to that cross, declaring with His final breath, "It is finished."

The Final Words from the Cross

It is crucial to understand Jesus' final words from the cross. They were intentional and significant. Each phrase was not only powerful, but also ordered with purpose:

1. A prayer to the Father—*"Father, forgive them, for they know not what they do" (Luke 23:34).*

2. A pardon to the sinner—*"Remember Me" (Matthew 23:42-43).*

3. Passing responsibility to a friend—*"Woman, behold your son; Son, behold your mother"* (John 19:25-27).

4. Passing blame—*"My God, My God, why have you forsaken me?"* (Matthew 27:46).

5. A personal statement of humanity—*"I thirst"* (John 19:28).

6. The declaration of completion—*"It is finished"* (John 19:30).

7. Surrender—*"Into your hands I commit my spirit"* (Luke 23:46).

Notice that Jesus addresses the Father three times—at the beginning, middle, and end. This emphasizes His relationship with the Father throughout His suffering. When He uttered, "I thirst," it was a personal statement to remind us that He was fully human. He experienced pain, misunderstanding, betrayal, and loneliness, just as we do. You are never alone in your struggles.

When Jesus proclaimed, "It is finished," He used the Greek word *tetelestai*, which signifies the complete cancellation of a debt. He didn't say, "I am finished," but rather proclaimed victory over sin and death. Jesus declared that the debt owed to the Father was wiped away completely. This wasn't about His debts but the debts of humankind, the debt of sin. This declaration echoed throughout the heavens and hell, ringing true for all to hear.

In that moment, Satan's stronghold over humanity was shattered. Hebrews 2:14 reminds us, "Since the children have flesh and blood, he too shared in their humanity so that by his death he might break the power of him who holds the power of death—that is, the devil."

Are you living under the power of sin? There's a significant difference between falling short and living in a pattern of sin. You may feel trapped by your family history or past mistakes. But here's the good news: God can alter your genes and change your story. Jesus is on the main line; just tell Him what you want!

Personal Reflection

1. Reflect on Your Debt: Take a moment to identify any areas in your life where you feel indebted, whether it's emotional burdens, relational conflicts, or even past sins. Acknowledge them before God, understanding that Jesus has declared, "It is finished," over those debts.

   _____

   _____

2. Speak Life: This week, practice using your words to declare freedom and victory. Whenever you feel overwhelmed by circumstances, remind yourself that you are a child of God. Use affirmations based on Scripture to reinforce your identity in Christ.

   _____

   _____

3. Identify Strongholds: Think about the areas where you feel trapped. Write down the specific struggles you face— whether they are doubts, fears, or patterns of sin. Pray over them, declaring that today, in the name of Jesus, those strongholds are finished!

   _____

   _____

4. Community Engagement: Consider who you might be stepping over in your daily life—those in need of support, compassion, or even just a friendly smile. How can you be a source of encouragement or assistance to those around you? Commit to being more aware of those needs and respond in love.

   _____

   _____

Conclusion

There is a divine completion in the declaration, "It is finished." It involves the Father, the Son, and the Holy Spirit working together in our lives. Remember, you are not alone, and your debt has been paid in full. Embrace the freedom that comes from Jesus' sacrifice and let His power transform every aspect of your life.

PRAYER

Heavenly Father, Thank You for the incredible gift of salvation through Jesus. Thank You that He declared, "It is finished," and paid the debt for my sins. Help me to recognize the power in my words and the authority I have as Your child. Teach me to speak life into my circumstances and to break every chain that holds me back. May I lean on You for strength and guidance, knowing that my story can change because of You. In Jesus' mighty name, I pray. Amen.

DAY 30:

LET YOUR LIGHT SHINE: THE LEGACY OF JOSEPH

Scripture: Matthew 1:20-25

"But after he had considered this, an angel of the Lord appeared to him in a dream and said, 'Joseph son of David, do not be afraid to take Mary home as your wife, because what is conceived in her is from the Holy Spirit. She will give birth to a son, and you are to give him the name Jesus, because he will save his people from their sins.'"

Introduction

The ordinary man who became extraordinary: Joseph. In Matthew's account, we encounter Joseph, an ordinary man who played a pivotal role in an extraordinary story. Let's take a closer look at his life. Joseph's lineage connected him to King David, a fulfillment of prophecy. His heritage was significant, showing God's meticulous planning through generations. His trade as a carpenter illustrates his hardworking nature. He built with his hands and nurtured a skill that would provide for his family.

Joseph was chosen to be the earthly father of Jesus. What an immense honor and responsibility that must have been! A man of great values and integrity: The Bible describes him as a "just man." He exemplified righteousness and fairness, even in difficult situations.

The Bible doesn't tell the whole story of Joseph. We often wonder— if Joseph had known the entire story upfront, would he have accepted the call? Yet, God assures us that He never puts more on us than we can bear. Joseph demonstrated faith even in the unknown. Joseph trusted and obeyed God's plan, showing us the importance of faith in our own lives.

Despite Jesus not being his biological son, Joseph embraced his role wholeheartedly. He is a powerful example of love, care, and responsibility. Joseph exemplified wisdom in his decisions. He was slow to anger, choosing kindness over retribution, embodying the principle of loving one's enemies.

We are Chosen

In God's hands, the ordinary can become extraordinary. Just like Joseph, we have the potential to be called just and valued for our character and integrity. The Bible doesn't reveal much about Joseph, yet the little it does say remains impactful even today. Not all of us will achieve fame or widespread recognition, but for those who cross our paths, let's strive to leave a meaningful mark.

Our legacy should be rooted in a deep love for God that sets a foundation for all else. Let your life be a testament to unwavering faith in God's promises. Every interaction is an opportunity to show kindness and dignity. Live in a way that reflects the extraordinary nature of God's grace in your life.

Personal Reflection

During this season in your life, consider how you can embody the qualities of Joseph in your daily life. Here are some practical steps:

1. Show Kindness to Others: Take a moment to check in on friends, family, or even neighbors. A simple message or phone call can brighten someone's day.

   _____

   _____

2. Embrace Your Role: Whether as a parent, friend, spouse, or colleague, recognize the importance of your role in the lives of those around you. Approach it with love and commitment.

   _____

   _____

3. Practice Patience and Integrity: In challenging situations, remind yourself to respond as Joseph did—with wisdom and grace. Take a deep breath and choose to act kindly, even when provoked.

   _____

   _____

4. Leave a Lasting Impact: Reflect on your own legacy. What do you want people to remember about you? Consider how your actions today contribute to that legacy.

   _____

   _____

5. Cultivate a Spirit of Worship: Like Joseph, stay connected to God through prayer and worship. Let your relationship with Him guide your actions and interactions.

   _____

   _____

Conclusion

This season, let us be inspired by Joseph's example. May we embrace our roles, trust in God's plan, and leave a legacy of love and integrity. Let your light shine brightly, for it can illuminate the path for others as we reflect the love of Jesus in our actions and words.

PRAYER

Heavenly Father, thank You for the example of Joseph, who shows me how to live with faith and integrity. Help me to shine my light in the world, treating everyone with love and respect. May my life reflect Your grace and goodness, leaving a lasting impact on those around me. In Jesus' name, I pray. Amen.

DAY 31:

JOY TO THE WORLD: THE GIFT OF JOY

Scripture: Psalms 98

*"Oh, sing to the L*ORD *a new song! For He has done marvelous things; His right hand and His holy arm have gained Him the victory. 2 The L*ORD *has made known His salvation; His righteousness He has revealed in the sight of the [a]nations. 3 He has remembered His mercy and His faithfulness to the house of Israel; All the ends of the earth have seen the salvation of our God."*

Introduction

The beautiful carol "Joy to the World" is one of my favorite holiday songs. Penned by Isaac Watts in 1719, Psalm 98 inspired it. This psalm invites us to sing a new song to the Lord, celebrating His marvelous works and the salvation He has revealed to all nations. The joyful proclamation of Jesus' birth calls us to anticipate the day when sin will be vanquished, and we will bask in God's righteousness.

The concept of joy resonates deeply within Scripture. In the English Standard Version, the words "joy," "rejoice," or "joyful" appear a staggering 430 times, emphasizing that joy is far more enduring than mere happiness. While happiness can be fleeting, joy satisfies the heart in profound and lasting ways.

Joy in Scripture:

- Psalm 32:11: "Be glad in the Lord, and rejoice, O righteous, and shout for joy, all you upright in heart!"
- Philippians 4:4: "Rejoice in the Lord always; again, I will say, rejoice."
- Romans 12:12: "Rejoice in hope, be patient in tribulation, be constant in prayer."
- Galatians 5:22-23: "The fruit of the Spirit includes joy as a fundamental characteristic of a life lived in Christ."
- 1 Peter 1:8: "Though you have not seen him, you love him. Though you do not now see him, you believe in him and rejoice with joy that is inexpressible and filled with glory."

Finding Joy

For me, joy is not just a concept; it's a lived experience, deeply influenced by my mother's faith and her ability to find joy in all circumstances. She taught me that joy is not dependent on our situations but comes from our relationship with God.

It's easy to rejoice when life is going well. But what about when challenges arise? I remember a time when a friend at work was struggling. I tried to help but felt overwhelmed by life myself. It was in those moments that I learned not to let my circumstances dictate my praise. A relationship with Jesus transforms our perspective. Philippians 4:6-7 reminds us to bring our worries to God through prayer, resulting in a peace that surpasses understanding. Surrounding ourselves with uplifting people also cultivates joy in our lives.

Let's break down what JOY can mean for you:

- Jesus Over Yourself: Prioritize your relationship with Jesus more than anything else.

- Jesus Others Yourself: Serve and uplift others, reflecting Christ's love in tangible ways.

- Just Overcome Yourself: Recognize and move past your own challenges for the sake of bringing joy to others.

Let's set aside self and embrace the joy of giving and serving. Jesus invites us to ask in His name, promising that our joy may be full (John 16:24). In a world filled with doubt, our joy is rooted in the assurance that we serve a risen Savior.

I remember growing up singing the hymn, "He Lives." The hymn says, "I serve a risen Savior, He's in the world today." His presence is a source of joy that reassures us, no matter our circumstances. He walks with us along life's narrow way, providing comfort and companionship. He is alive today!

Personal Reflection

As we reflect on the joy that Jesus brings, let's focus on practical ways to embody this joy in our daily lives. Here are some personal applications for you to consider:

1. Daily Gratitude: Write three things you're grateful for. This simple practice can shift your focus from challenges to blessings, fostering a joyful heart.

   _____

   _____

2. Joyful Conversations: Engage in conversations that uplift, and encourage. Share a testimony of God's goodness and joy in your life. Surrounding yourself with positivity can create an environment of joy.

   _____

   _____

3. Worship Through Song: Spend time singing praises, whether at home or at church. Let the lyrics of joyful songs fill your heart and mind, reminding you of God's faithfulness and love.

_____

_____

By implementing these practices, we can actively spread joy in our communities, shining the light of Jesus in a world that desperately needs it. Let's make today a time of joyful connection, celebration, and service, reminding ourselves and others of the faith we have and finding hope in Jesus.

Conclusion

As we celebrate this joyful season, let us reflect on the profound joy that Jesus brings into our lives. May we be inspired by the message of "Joy to the World," singing and proclaiming the joy of our Savior. Let us choose joy daily, serving others and sharing the love of Christ in all we do.

PRAYER

Heavenly Father, thank You for the joy that comes from knowing You. Help me to share that joy with others this season. May my life reflect the light of Christ, bringing hope and encouragement to those around me. Let me rejoice always, in every circumstance, knowing that You are with me. In Jesus' name, I pray. Amen.

DAY 32:

REDEEMED

Scripture: 1 Kings 22:48

"Now Jehoshaphat built a fleet of trading ships to go to Ophir for gold, but they never set sail—they were wrecked at Ezion Geber. 49 At that time Ahaziah son of Ahab said to Jehoshaphat, 'Let my men sail with yours,' but Jehoshaphat refused."

Introduction

In this verse, we find a poignant reference to ships that never sailed, echoing the heart-wrenching stories of lives cut short before their potential could be realized. Reflecting on my time as a mentor in a housing project, I began to understand the depth of what it means to judge others without knowing their stories.

Harsh Realities

Growing up in the country, I thought my struggles were significant, but as I entered this low-income community, I realized that others faced challenges far greater. I learned not to judge a book by its cover; my willingness to listen opened doors to understanding the real issues at hand—families torn apart by incarceration, addiction, and loss.

Through my conversations, I encountered the harsh realities that many in the community grappled with: sons and daughters in jail, families shattered by drug addiction, and single-parent homes aching for support. I began to hear questions and statements both from those in the community and spectators that often lingered in the air. They carried weight because they were rooted in misunderstanding and judgment:

> "Why don't they just leave the neighborhood?"
>
> "Why is there so much black-on-black crime?"
>
> "When they pull you over, just be respectful and don't ask questions."
>
> "They don't want to work, instead, they just milk the system."

These questions and statements were answered not by words, but by the stories of resilience and pain I heard from the community. They reminded me of the scripture in 1 Kings, where we see a new king, Jehoshaphat, facing a divided kingdom, striving to make a difference in the midst of challenges.

The Tragedy of Ships That Never Sailed

The ships wrecked before they could even set sail. There's nothing more heartbreaking than potential unfulfilled, dreams unrealized. This was certainly the case in the community that I was working in. All their ships were wrecked before they could sail.

When ships wreck in port, we must consider the reasons why. There are external threats, like pirates—representing Satan—who seek to destroy without regard for the lives involved. Then there are saboteurs, individuals or systems that benefit from others' struggles, and internal factors, like whether their foundations were secure.

Just as a ship needs a strong tabernacle to withstand storms, we need to be rooted in God's word. Are we tightly anchored in our faith? If we aren't, we risk capsizing when life's storms hit. But when our foundation is strong, we can face adversity with confidence.

It's crucial to surround ourselves with the right crew—people who lift us up, who can navigate the storms alongside us, who remind us that we are not alone. Sometimes, we need to let go of those who drag us down, even if it's painful.

Even if a ship sinks, there's hope in the form of salvage ships— those dedicated to rescuing what seems lost. These vessels venture where others will not, seeking to restore and redeem. They don't recognize borders; their mission is to save.

Maritime history teaches us that when a wrecked ship is salvaged, it can be rebuilt with some of its original parts, turning past failures into a testimony of triumph. We are called to be like those salvage ships, working to redeem what the world sees as lost.

As we reflect on our journey, let us remember that each salvaged ship carries a plaque with one powerful word: "Redeem." This signifies not just restoration, but the acknowledgment of a story that was once fractured, now whole again.

Jehoshaphat's Radical Vision

Jehoshaphat's situation was dire; his kingdom was economically strained after the previous king had spent resources on war. Instead of succumbing to despair, he adopted a "Yes We Can" attitude. He resolved to build ships in the desert—a radical move that symbolized hope and possibility. Despite the lack of visible resources, Jehoshaphat saw potential in the people and the land.

Building ships in the desert didn't make sense, yet it represented a vision for a future filled with opportunities. In the same way, we can choose to build hope in our communities, even when it seems impossible. Jehoshaphat wanted to provide for his people and offer them new possibilities, just as God often does for us.

Personal Reflection

1. Reflecting on my own experiences, I recognize that each of us carries stories shaped by our backgrounds and encounters. Think about your journey—what struggles have you faced? How have they informed your perspective? In my role as a mentor, I learned the importance of empathy and listening. I encourage you to take time to connect with those in your community. Ask questions, listen deeply, and strive to understand the complexities of their lives.

   _____

   _____

2. Consider the "ships" in your life—what dreams or goals do you have that may feel stalled or wrecked? Are there relationships or aspirations that seem stuck in port? Identify them, and reflect on the factors that may be holding them back. Are there internal doubts or external influences that you need to confront?

   _____

   _____

3. Evaluate the strength of your foundation. Are you anchored in faith and the truth of God's Word? Spend time in prayer and scripture to ensure that you're rooted and equipped to face life's storms. Strengthen your spiritual tabernacle by participating in community worship and studying the Bible with others.

   _____

   _____

Conclusion

Let's commit to being the change we wish to see. Let's work together to uplift and redeem our communities. In doing so, we can honor the legacy of those who came before us while building a future filled with hope, possibility, and unity. Remember, as we seek to redeem our own lives and the lives of others, we carry a powerful message of hope and transformation. Just as the salvage of a ship brings new life to wrecked vessels, we can bring redemption to the lives around us. Let's carry the spirit of "Redeem" in our hearts and actions, knowing that every story matters and every life has value.

PRAYER

Lord, thank You for the gift of redemption and the call to uplift one another. Help me to listen, learn, and support each other, recognizing the value in every story. May I work with others to build bridges of understanding and compassion. In Jesus' name, Amen.

DAY 33:

THE WALK TO THE CROSS

Scripture: Mark 15:1-15

"Very early in the morning, the chief priests, with the elders, the teachers of the law and the whole Sanhedrin, made their plans. So they bound Jesus, led him away and handed him over to Pilate."

Introduction

The journey Jesus took to the cross was not just a path of suffering, but a journey of love, sacrifice, and redemption. Every step He took, every word He spoke, and every miracle He performed pointed to the ultimate purpose of His life: to be the sacrificial Lamb for the sins of the world. There were significant moments of His life and the final hours leading to His crucifixion, highlighting what His sacrifice means for us today.

What Jesus Teaches Us

From the very beginning, Jesus' life was extraordinary, better than any blockbuster movie! He was conceived by the Holy Spirit and born of the Virgin Mary; His birth fulfilled prophecies and signaled the arrival of the promised Messiah. Even before He was born, His life was sought after by those who feared His purpose. At a young age, Jesus was found in the temple, discussing the Scriptures with the teachers. He knew His purpose and was committed to it from the start.

Remember the wedding in Cana, where Jesus turned water into wine? He revealed His divine authority and began His public ministry. Jesus demonstrated His power over nature, showing that He is Lord over all creation. His authority over demonic forces revealed His power to set people free from spiritual bondage. With just a touch of His garment, a woman who had suffered for twelve years was healed. Her faith and His compassion met, resulting in her healing.

With five loaves and two fish, Jesus fed a multitude, illustrating His ability to provide abundantly and miraculously. With just a command, He calmed the raging sea, reminding us that even the winds and waves obey Him. Jesus cleansed the temple, overturning tables and driving out those who had turned His Father's house into a marketplace. Jesus showed His humanity and compassion when He wept at the tomb of Lazarus, even though He knew He would raise him from the dead.

He called his good friend Lazarus out of the grave, demonstrating His power over death itself. Judas, one of His disciples, betrayed Him for thirty pieces of silver. This act of betrayal led to Jesus' arrest and crucifixion, reminding us not to put our trust in man alone.

Peter, one of His closest disciples, denied knowing Him three times. Yet, Jesus' love and forgiveness restored Peter, showing us that failure is not the end when we turn back to God.

Pilate, though recognizing Jesus' innocence, bowed to the pressure of the crowd. Jesus was flogged, mocked, and crowned with thorns. The soldiers struck Him repeatedly and dressed Him in a purple robe, mocking His kingship. Exhausted and in pain, He could barely carry the cross. As Jesus struggled under the weight of the cross, Simon of Cyrene was compelled to help Him carry it. What an honor and a burden it must have been to carry the cross of the Savior.

1. The Power of Support: Jesus needed help, showing us that it's okay to need others. We weren't meant to walk this journey alone.

2. The Honor of Carrying the Cross: Simon's act reminds us that sometimes we are called to step in and carry the burdens of others, reflecting Christ's love in tangible ways.

3. Community in Faith: Having someone to lean on during tough times is crucial. God places people in our lives to support us, and He calls us to do the same for others.

Nailed to the Cross

With each nail driven into His hands and feet, Jesus endured unimaginable pain. The cross wasn't just an instrument of death, but a symbol of the greatest love the world has ever known.

1. One for the Father: Jesus, the Son, was sent by the Father to redeem humanity.

2. One for the Son: He willingly laid down His life for our sins.

3. One for the Holy Spirit: The Spirit empowers us to live out the victory that Jesus won on the cross.

On either side of Jesus hung two thieves. One mocked Him, but the other, recognizing Jesus' innocence, asked to be remembered in His kingdom. Jesus, even in His agony, extended grace and promised him paradise. Jesus' response to the repentant thief shows us that it's never too late to turn to Him. Even in His suffering, Jesus asked the Father to forgive those who crucified Him, demonstrating the depth of His love and mercy.

When Jesus gave up His spirit, the earth shook, and the temple veil was torn in two. His death signified the end of the old covenant and the beginning of a new way for us to be reconciled to God. Jesus'

death freed us from the bondage of sin and opened the way for us to have a personal relationship with God. Romans 5:8 reminds us that while we were still sinners, Christ died for us. His love is not based on our worthiness, but on His grace.

Personal Reflection

1. What does the cross mean to you personally?

   _____

   _____

2. How does it impact the way you live your life?

   _____

   _____

3. Have you ever faced mockery or unjust treatment for your faith? How did you respond?

   _____

   _____

Conclusion

Anyone might lay down their life for a loved one, but Jesus laid down His life for those who despised and rejected Him. He died not just for His friends, but for His enemies. The walk to the cross was filled with pain and suffering, but it was also a journey of purpose and victory. Jesus' sacrifice has opened the way for us to experience eternal life and reconciliation with God. The cross is not just a symbol of death, but a beacon of hope, love, and redemption.

PRAYER

Lord, thank You for Your unimaginable love and sacrifice on the cross. Help me to trust You more deeply, to forgive as You forgave, and to love as You loved. May the message of the cross transform my heart and guide my life. In Jesus' name, Amen.

DAY 34:

ARE YOU THIRSTY?

Scripture: John 4:7-15

"When a Samaritan woman came to draw water, Jesus said to her, 'Will you give me a drink?'"

Introduction

The story of the Samaritan woman at the well is one of the most profound encounters in the Bible. It's not just a story of Jesus helping someone in need; it's an unveiling of who He truly is. Through His conversation with this woman, Jesus reveals the depth of His love, the power of His grace, and His desire to meet us at our point of need, no matter where we are or what we've done. This chapter explores what it means to have a thirst that only Jesus can quench and the transformation that takes place when we encounter Him.

Outcasts

Jesus was traveling from Judea to Galilee, a journey of about seventy miles. The Bible tells us He "had to go through Samaria." He stopped in a town called Sychar, about forty miles into His journey. It was the middle of the day, and Jesus, weary from His travels, rested by a well. This wasn't just a chance stop; it was a divine appointment.

A Samaritan woman came to draw water, and Jesus did something no other Jew would do: He spoke to her. In that time, Jews despised Samaritans, considering them half-breeds due to their mixed heritage of Israelites and Assyrians. The animosity was so intense that a Jew would avoid crossing paths with a Samaritan, even avoiding their shadows if they crossed. For a Jewish man, especially a Rabbi, to speak to a Samaritan woman was unheard of.

This woman was not just any woman; she was an outcast even among her own people. She came to the well at noon, the hottest part of the day, to avoid the other women who would come in the cool of the morning or evening. This indicates that she was shunned and judged by her community. Jesus met her where she was, in her isolation and shame.

Despite these barriers, Jesus initiated a conversation. He didn't let societal norms or prejudices stop Him from reaching out to her. He offered her something no one else could: living water. Jesus offered her "living water," a concept that must have sounded confusing. She came for physical water, but He spoke of a spiritual thirst only He could quench. Her response was practical: "You have nothing to draw with, and the well is deep." How often do we, like her, focus on the physical, the tangible, and the immediate, missing the greater spiritual reality?

Jesus' words were designed to stir her curiosity and draw her deeper into conversation. He wanted her to see beyond the surface and understand the deeper need within her soul. The woman expressed her desire for the water Jesus offered, but Jesus didn't stop there. He asked her to call her husband. Her response, "I have no husband," opened the door for Jesus to reveal her deeper need. She had been married five times and was now living with a man who wasn't her husband. Jesus wasn't trying to shame her; He was bringing her brokenness to light so He could heal it.

The woman's story reflects a cycle of brokenness and disappointment. In her time, only men could initiate divorce, and for reasons as trivial as a disfigurement or inability to cook. She had been promised love and stability five times, only to be let down each time. Now, she was with a man, but not married, trying to avoid more heartbreak and social disgrace. Like her, we often go back to dry wells, hoping they will one day satisfy us. She wasn't just thirsting for water; she was thirsting for acceptance, love, and purpose.

When Jesus confronted her with the truth, she tried to change the subject, bringing up a theological debate about where to worship. But Jesus cut through the distraction, emphasizing that true worship is not about a place, but about worshiping in spirit and truth. The woman spoke of the Messiah, saying, "When He comes, He will explain to us." Jesus' response was powerful: "I, the one speaking to you—I am He." For the first time, Jesus explicitly revealed His identity as the Messiah. This revelation, given to a woman, a Samaritan, an outcast, underscores His love and grace for the marginalized.

The woman left her water jar and went back to her town, telling everyone about her encounter with Jesus. She who came to the well in shame now boldly proclaimed her testimony, leading many to believe in Jesus.

Personal Reflection

1. What are you thirsting for in your life right now? How have you tried to satisfy that thirst? What is it that you need to bring to Jesus?

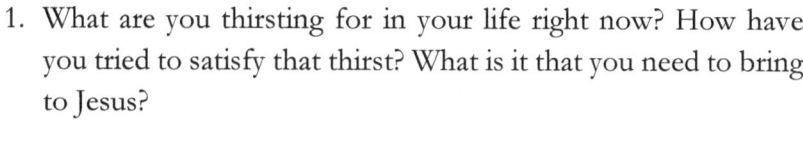

2. What are the things in your life that you have been avoiding or hiding? What "wells" have you been returning to in search of satisfaction? Are they leaving you thirstier than before?

_____

_____

3. How often do we deflect when God tries to address a deep issue in our lives? What masks are you wearing that you need to take off in order to worship in spirit and truth?

_____

_____

Conclusion

Jesus is still meeting people at their wells, still offering living water that satisfies the deepest thirsts of our souls. Whatever you are thirsting for, know that He is the source. He is the answer. He is the living water.

PRAYER

Lord, thank You for meeting me at my well, for seeing beyond my facade and loving me anyway. Help me to drink deeply of the living water You offer, to be satisfied in You alone. Break the cycles of brokenness in my life and fill me with Your Spirit. May I worship You in spirit and in truth and share the living water with others. In Jesus' name, Amen.

DAY 35:

CHAOS TO CALM

Scripture: Mark 4:35-41

"Then He arose and rebuked the wind, and said to the sea,
"Peace,[a] be still!" And the wind ceased and there was a great calm.
40 But He said to them, 'Why are you so fearful? How[b] is it that
you have no faith?' 41 And they feared exceedingly, and said to one
another, 'Who can this be, that even the wind and the
sea obey Him!'"

Introduction

Have you ever been caught in a storm? Think back to Hurricane Hugo in 1989—an event that brought destruction, confusion, and turmoil. Chaos surrounded everything, leaving people in a state of disorder and distress. This is the nature of chaos: overwhelming, unpredictable, and unsettling.

Chaos is a state of utter confusion and disorder. It manifests in misunderstandings, emotional turmoil, and the disruptions of life. In contrast, calm is the absence of fear, the presence of peace, and the ability to rest even during a storm.

In Mark 4:35-41, the disciples faced a violent storm while Jesus slept peacefully in the boat. Overcome with fear, they woke Him, exclaiming, "Teacher, do You not care that we are perishing?" (Mark 4:38). Yet, in one moment, with three powerful words— "Peace, be still"— Jesus calmed the storm.

What More Can We Learn from Jesus?

The disciples' reaction in the storm mirrors how we often respond to chaos in our lives. Fear and panic consume us, and we question whether God sees or cares. But Jesus demonstrated the power of faith over fear. He was able to sleep because His trust in the Father was unwavering.

1. Faith Brings Rest – Jesus could sleep in the storm because He knew who was in control. When our faith is strong, our hearts can remain at peace even when life is turbulent.

2. Chaos Can't Overcome Christ – No matter how overwhelming life feels, nothing is beyond God's authority. The storm obeyed His command, and so will the storms in your life.

3. Stillness is a Choice – Psalm 46:10 reminds us, "Be still, and know that I am God." We must practice stillness and trust in His sovereignty.

Many times, our natural reaction is to try to fix the chaos ourselves. We seek temporary relief—distractions, self-reliance, or even avoidance. But Jesus invites us to surrender and rest in Him. Instead of fighting the storm, we can learn to trust in the One who has the power to calm it.

Personal Reflection

1. What storms are you facing right now? Financial uncertainty, relationship struggles, health concerns?

   _____

   _____

2. Are you reacting like the disciples—fearful and doubting— or like Jesus—trusting and resting?

   _____

   _____

3. What practical steps can you take to be still and allow God to work in your situation?

   _____

   _____

4. Take a moment to reflect: If Jesus could rest in the storm, why can't we? What would it look like to truly trust Him in the middle of your chaos?

   _____

   _____

Conclusion

Jesus asked His disciples, "Why are you so fearful? How is it that you have no faith?" (Mark 4:40). Their fear was a sign of their lack of trust in Him. But Jesus desires that we move from fear to faith, from chaos to calm.

God is not absent in your storm. He is right there in the boat with you, ready to bring peace. The question is: Will you trust Him enough to rest, or will you continue striving in fear?

When we truly believe that God is in control, we can surrender our anxieties, quiet our hearts, and embrace His perfect peace.

PRAYER

Father, in the midst of my storms, help me to trust You. When chaos surrounds me, remind me that You are in control. Teach me to be still and rest in Your presence, knowing that You are my refuge and strength. Just as Jesus calmed the storm, I ask that You speak peace into my heart and my circumstances. Increase my faith, Lord, so that I may walk in confidence, knowing that You are with me. In Jesus' name, Amen.

DAY 36:

TASTE AND SEE: SAVORING GOD'S GOODNESS

Scripture: Psalm 34:8

"Taste and see that the Lord is good; blessed is the one who takes refuge in Him."

Introduction

Imagine sitting at a table filled with a feast of the most delicious, fragrant, and satisfying food. The aroma fills the air, and everything looks incredible. But what if you never took a bite? What if you only admired the food from a distance, but never experienced the flavors for yourself?

This is what happens when we acknowledge God's goodness, but don't fully experience it in our daily lives. The invitation in Psalm 34:8 isn't just to know that God is good—it's to taste and see His goodness firsthand. It's an invitation to a deep, personal experience with Him, one that satisfies the soul and leaves us wanting more.

The Feast All Around Us

Food is essential for survival. It nourishes, sustains, and strengthens us. But imagine if you only took small, occasional bites—never eating enough to be truly full. Spiritually, many of us live this way. We nibble on God's Word when it's convenient. We sip on His promises when we feel like it. But we don't always feast on His presence.

God invites us to fully experience Him. He wants us to indulge in His goodness, trusting that He is more than enough to satisfy our every need.

1. Taste – This requires action. Just like you can't taste food without putting it in your mouth, you can't experience God's goodness without seeking Him. We must be intentional— reading His Word, praying, and trusting Him daily.

2. See – Once we taste, our eyes are opened to how amazing He truly is. When we experience His faithfulness in small things, we recognize it in bigger moments. Our perspective shifts, and we start seeing evidence of His goodness everywhere.

Think about the times in your life when you've felt spiritually hungry. Maybe you were searching for peace, joy, or purpose. The truth is nothing else truly satisfies like God. We often try to fill ourselves with temporary things—success, relationships, entertainment—but they leave us empty. Only God provides lasting fulfillment.

When we sit at His table, we receive:

- Provision – He gives us what we need (Philippians 4:19).
- Peace – He calms our hearts (John 14:27).
- Joy – He fills us with His presence (Psalm 16:11).
- Strength – He sustains us when we are weak (Isaiah 40:31).

Personal Reflection

1. Evaluate Your Spiritual Diet – Are you truly feasting on God's Word, or just taking small bites?

   _____

   _____

2. Be Intentional – Set aside time to experience His goodness through prayer, worship, and Scripture.

   _____

   _____

3. Look for His Goodness – Keep a gratitude journal to recognize His faithfulness daily.

   _____

   _____

Conclusion

If you've been living on spiritual "snacks," it's time to pull up a chair and feast on God's goodness. God's goodness isn't just something to hear about—it's something to experience. Will you take a seat at His table today?

PRAYER

Lord, I don't want to just know about Your goodness—I want to experience it fully. Help me to taste and see that You are more than enough for me. Remove anything that keeps me from sitting at Your table and receiving what You have for me. Satisfy my soul with Your presence and let my life reflect the joy of knowing You. In Jesus' name, Amen.

DAY 37:

CROSSING THE GOAL LINE

Scripture: 2 Timothy 4:7-8

"I have fought the good fight, I have finished the race, I have kept the faith. Finally, there is laid up for me the crown of righteousness, which the Lord, the righteous Judge, will give to me on that Day, and not to me only but also to all who have loved His appearance."

Introduction

On January 31, 1988, over seventy-three thousand fans filled the stadium to witness a monumental game led by quarterback Doug Williams. The thrill of the game, the tension of the plays, and the roar of the crowd all encapsulate the spirit of competition and perseverance. Today, I invite you to consider your spiritual journey through the lens of the game of football.

The Offense vs Defense

I discovered my love for football while growing up in the country in South Carolina. I spent many afternoons and long summer days in our makeshift football field, which was my front yard or the side yard of my cousin's house. It wasn't until I played middle school football that I found I loved to tackle and hit people. Little did I know how my journey and love for football would shape my life for where I am today. Learning and developing in football taught me the transferable skills needed for life.

I played defense. My position in football was middle linebacker. My job was to stop the ball from advancing, gaining yards, or scoring a touchdown. I especially loved when I could sack the quarterback. As the team captain, my defensive coaches would tell me what plays to run, and it was my job to share it with the team and execute. Our whole job was to figure out ways to stop the plays, stop the score, stop them from being successful.

In football, the roles of the offense and defense are essentially a battle of tactics and skills. Simply put, the offense and defense are in a constant struggle for control of the game. The offense seeks to gain yardage and score points, while the defense aims to halt their progress and turn the tide in their favor. Every successful football team comprises various players, each with a distinct role, contributing to the overall goal. In our spiritual lives, we too have a team:

- The Coach: God, our true Legend, guiding us like a shepherd (Psalm 23).
- The Playbook: The Bible, our essential guide. As 2 Timothy 2:15 reminds us, "Study to show thyself approved unto God."
- The Quarterback (QB): Jesus, who leads by example. John 13:15 tells us, "I have set the example, and you should do for each other exactly what I have done for you."

Every team faces opposition. In our case, the enemy seeks to disrupt our progress. They hate our Coach, our QB, and most importantly, they hate us because we are part of God's team. The Holy Spirit acts as our referee, guiding and reminding us of the rules we must follow. Just as in football, we encounter penalties in life:

- False Start: Moving ahead of God's timing.
- Delay of Game: Hesitating when we should act.
- Pass Interference: Allowing distractions to sidetrack us.
- Unnecessary Roughness: Fighting battles on our own.

None of us is perfect. Proverbs 24:16 reminds us that "For a righteous man may fall seven times and rise again." It's not our mistakes that define us, but how we respond to them. We will fumble; we will stumble. Life is full of ups and downs. But when we're struggling, our community—our "village"—will notice and surround us with support and prayers. Football is a game of inches, and our spiritual journey is no different. Every step we take matters. The ultimate goal is the end zone—the touchdown of heaven! As Paul expresses in 2 Timothy 4:7-8, we strive to hear the words, "Well done, good and faithful servant!" It is the journey, the struggles, and the victories that bring us to this point.

Personal Reflection

As you consider your own spiritual journey, ask yourself:

1. Who is on your team? Reflect on the people who support and guide you in your faith.

   _____

   _____

2. What role do you play? Think about how you contribute to the body of Christ. Are you actively serving or seeking ways to get involved?

   _____

   _____

3. How do you handle setbacks? When you stumble, do you retreat, or do you lean on your community for support?

_____

_____

4. What inches can you gain today? Identify small, actionable steps you can take to move closer to your goals—whether it's prayer, Bible study, or reaching out to others.

_____

_____

Conclusion

Crossing the goal line requires effort, perseverance, and teamwork. Let us strive together, fighting the good fight, finishing the race, and keeping the faith. As you do, remain mindful of the crown of righteousness awaiting you. Remember, God has equipped you for the journey ahead—run with purpose!

PRAYER

Heavenly Father, thank You for the gift of community and for each role within Your body. Help me to stay focused on the goal and to encourage one another as I navigate the challenges in my life. May I cross the finish line together, united in faith. Amen.

DAY 38:

INVESTING WHAT GOD HAS GIVEN YOU

Scripture: Matthew 25:14-30

"For the kingdom of heaven is like a man traveling to a far country, who called his own servants and delivered his goods to them... To one he gave five talents, to another two, and to another one, to each according to his ability."

Introduction

What do we do with what God has given us? Do we use our gifts boldly, or do we hold back in fear? In Matthew 25, Jesus tells the parable of the talents, a story about three servants who were entrusted with different amounts of money. Two of them invested and multiplied what they received, but one buried his talent out of fear. His lack of action cost him everything.

This story isn't just about money—it's about faith, courage, and using the gifts God has given us.

The Investment

I can relate to this parable through an experience I had in high school. I played football, but honestly, I wasn't the best player on the field. I wasn't the fastest or the strongest, and I wasn't a natural- born star. But I was dedicated. I worked hard in practice, stayed disciplined, and showed up for my team.

One game, I got my chance to play. The coach put me in, and my heart was racing. I could have doubted myself, thinking, *What if I mess up? What if I don't measure up?* But instead, I gave everything I had. I ran my routes, played my position, and did my best. I wasn't perfect, but I didn't hold back.

Looking back, I see how God used that experience to teach me a greater lesson: He doesn't expect perfection, but He does expect faithfulness. The servant in the parable who buried his talent let fear hold him back. He worried about failing, so he did nothing. But God doesn't reward those who do nothing—He rewards those who trust Him enough to step out in faith.

How often do we hold back because we're afraid? Afraid of failing, afraid of what others will think, afraid that we aren't good enough? But God has given us gifts—whether it's our time, skills, resources, or influence—not to be hidden, but to be used for His glory.

Personal Reflection

1. Identify Your Talents – What gifts, skills, or opportunities has God given you? Are you using them, or are you hesitating out of fear?

   _____

   _____

2. Step Out in Faith – Don't wait until you feel "ready" or "good enough." God blesses those who take action with what they have.

_____

_____

3. Let Go of Fear – The servant who buried his talent was motivated by fear. Ask God to replace your fear with faith so you can boldly use what He has entrusted to you.

_____

_____

4. Trust the Process – I wasn't the best player on the field, but I still gave my all. Remember that growth and success come through faithfulness, not instant perfection.

_____

_____

Conclusion

God has entrusted each of us with unique gifts, talents, and opportunities. Like the servants in Matthew 25:14-30, we have a choice—will we invest what He has given us for His glory, or will we bury our gifts out of fear or hesitation?

True faith is demonstrated in action. God calls us to step forward, trust Him, and use what we have to build His kingdom. It's not about how much we have, but how faithfully we use it. When we invest in His purposes, He multiplies our efforts in ways we never imagined.

Don't let fear or comparison hold you back. Whatever God has placed in your hands, use it boldly, knowing that He will bless your faithfulness. One day, may we all hear, "Well done, good and faithful servant."

PRAYER

Father, thank You for the gifts, talents, and opportunities You have given me. Help me to use them wisely and courageously, not allowing fear or doubt to hold me back. I trust that when I step out in faith, You will bless my efforts. May everything I do bring glory to You. In Jesus' name, Amen.

DAY 39:

PROCLAIMING THE CROSS

Scripture: John 3:16

"For God so loved the world that he gave his one and only Son, that whoever believes in him shall not perish but have eternal life."

Introduction

The cross is more than a symbol—it is the ultimate declaration of God's love and sacrifice for us. Too often, we take for granted what Jesus endured for our salvation. But when we truly reflect on the power of the cross, we realize that it calls us to something greater. It calls us to proclaim its truth boldly.

Love Through Action

Imagine standing at the foot of the cross, seeing Jesus hanging there, bruised and beaten. The weight of the world's sin pressed upon Him, yet in His pain, He proclaimed love, forgiveness, and redemption.

Proclaiming the cross is not just about speaking words—it's about living a life that reflects the sacrifice Jesus made. It means:

- Sharing the gospel unapologetically.
- Living in a way that honors His sacrifice.
- Showing love, grace, and forgiveness to others.

In John 3:16, God reveals His love through action. He *gave* His Son. He didn't just say He loved us—He demonstrated it through sacrifice. In the same way, proclaiming the cross is more than wearing a necklace or attending church; it's about demonstrating Christ's love daily.

The Story of "Checkmate"

In the Louvre Museum, there is a famous painting titled *Checkmate*. It depicts a man playing chess with Satan. The man appears defeated, looking down in despair as Satan grins, believing he has won. The title suggests that the game is over, and Satan has won.

However, a chess grandmaster once observed the painting carefully and noticed something striking. He exclaimed, *"The king still has one more move!"* The game was not over—the man still had a chance to turn things around.

This story powerfully illustrates the devil's greatest deception— making us believe we are defeated. He wants us to think that our sins, struggles, and failures mean we have lost the battle. But the truth is, because of the cross, the King always has one more move. Jesus' death and resurrection secured our victory over sin and death.

Satan thought the cross was his victory, but it was actually his greatest defeat. Jesus' sacrifice changed everything, and because of that, we are never without hope.

Personal Reflection

1. How are you proclaiming the cross in your daily life? Do your actions reflect the message of Christ's sacrifice?

    _____

    _____

2. Are you willing to be bold in sharing your faith? Sometimes, fear holds us back from talking about Jesus, but we are called to be His witnesses.

    _____

    _____

3. Are you living in defeat when the King still has one more move? No matter your struggle, Jesus' victory on the cross means there is always hope.

    _____

    _____

Let today be the day you commit to proclaiming the cross, not just in words, but in the way you live, love, and serve.

Conclusion

The message of the cross is the most excellent proclamation of love the world has ever known. John 3:16 reminds us that God's love is not just for a select few, but for everyone who believes in Him. Through Jesus' sacrifice, we have been given the gift of eternal life—an unshakable hope that transforms us from the inside out.

Proclaiming the cross is not just about words; it's about how we live our lives. It's in the grace we extend, the love we show, and the truth we stand upon. The enemy may try to convince us that our past disqualifies us or that we are not worthy of God's love, but the cross declares otherwise.

May we boldly live as witnesses of Christ, sharing His love and truth with a world in desperate need of hope. Let us never be ashamed of the gospel, for it is "the power of God that brings salvation to everyone who believes" (Romans 1:16).

PRAYER

Heavenly Father, thank You for the cross. Thank You for loving me so much that You gave Your Son to die in my place. Help me to live a life that proclaims Your love and sacrifice. Give me the boldness to share my faith and the wisdom to demonstrate Your grace in all that I do. When the enemy tries to deceive me into believing I am defeated, remind me that the King always has one more move. May my life reflect the power of the cross, leading others to You. In Jesus' name, Amen.

DAY 40:

DIG AND DUNG: A DEVOTIONAL ON GROWTH AND GRACE

Scripture: Luke 13:8

"'Sir,' the man replied, 'leave it alone for one more year, and I'll dig around it and fertilize it.'"

Introduction

Have you ever felt stuck in life, like you're not growing, producing, or living up to your full potential? There are seasons where we feel stagnant, overlooked, or even like a failure. But in Luke 13, Jesus tells the parable of the barren fig tree, a tree that was supposed to bear fruit, but remained lifeless. Instead of immediately cutting it down, the gardener pleads for more time. He promises to dig around it and apply fertilizer (dung), nurturing it back to life.

This story reminds us of God's grace and patience. He does not discard us when we struggle; instead, He works on us, giving us what we need to grow. Sometimes, that means digging into the hard places of our hearts and allowing the unpleasant "dung" of life— trials, discipline, and challenges—to fertilize our spiritual growth.

The Gifts of Discomfort

There was a time in my life when I felt buried under pressure, anxiety, and doubt. The weight of expectations, failures, and disappointments made me feel like I wasn't moving forward. But then, God reminded me that I wasn't buried—I was planted.

Just like in gardening, growth often requires uncomfortable conditions. The gardener in Jesus' parable didn't just leave the fig tree alone. He dug around it, loosening the soil that had hardened around its roots. He added fertilizer—something smelly, unpleasant, and unwanted, but necessary for nourishment.

In the same way, God allows certain hardships in our lives, not to destroy us, but to develop us. The difficulties we face—loss, rejection, failure, uncertainty—may feel like obstacles, but they are often the very things that push us toward deeper faith, stronger character, and greater dependence on Him.

Consider how God has been "digging and dunging" in your life:

- Has He been loosening the hardened areas of your heart?
- Is He using trials to strengthen your faith?
- Have you experienced situations that seemed like setbacks but were actually setups for growth?

God is patient with us. Even when we feel unproductive, He is working beneath the surface, preparing us to bear fruit.

Personal Reflection

1. Reflect on a time when you felt stuck or unfruitful. How did God nurture you during that season?

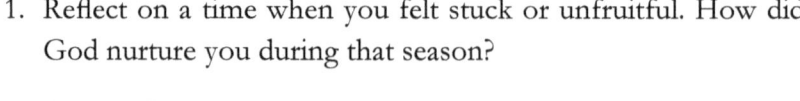

2. Identify an area in your life where you feel like you're experiencing "digging" or "dunging." Ask God to show you how He is using it for your good.

     _____

     _____

3. Instead of resisting hardships, pray for the grace to embrace them as part of God's process of growth in your life.

     _____

     _____

Conclusion

Growth takes time, and grace sustains us through the process. Just as the gardener in Jesus' parable was willing to dig around the tree and fertilize it, God is patient with us, nurturing us even when we feel unfruitful. He does not abandon us in our struggles, but lovingly tends to our hearts, cultivating the transformation He desires. There will be seasons when we feel stagnant or overlooked, but God sees the potential within us. His grace gives us another chance to grow, to bear fruit, and to walk in the purpose He has designed for us. Our responsibility is to remain open to His work, allowing Him to prune, nourish, and shape us into who we were created to be. No matter how barren your past may seem, God is still at work. Trust His process, embrace His grace, and step forward in faith. The season of fruitfulness will come.

PRAYER

Heavenly Father, thank You for Your patience and grace. Even when I feel stagnant, you are still working in me. Help me to trust Your process, even when it feels uncomfortable. Loosen the hardened places in my heart and use every challenge to shape me into who You've called me to be. I surrender to Your nurturing hands and that, in time, I will bear the fruit You desire. In Jesus' name, Amen.

CONCLUSION:

A FINAL WORD FOR YOUR JOURNEY

Dear Reader,

As you turn the final page of *Forty Days and Forty Nights*, we want to thank you for walking this journey with us. These devotionals were written from our hearts—rooted in Scripture, refined by life's storms, and carried by God's unfailing grace. Whether you've experienced loss, transition, or simply sought deeper connection with the Lord, our hope is that these forty reflections helped you find His peace—one day at a time.

But don't stop here.

Here are your action steps moving forward:

1. **Keep Showing Up** – Make time for God daily. Whether it's five minutes of silence or a full journaled prayer, show up and expect to meet Him there.

2. **Live What You've Learned** – Let what God stirred in your spirit lead to action. Walk in faith, speak life, forgive freely, and serve wholeheartedly. Be about His business.

3. **Share the Journey** – Encourage someone else. Share this devotional, start a group study, or simply be a listening ear. God uses our testimonies to touch others.

4. **Embrace the Next Forty** – The number forty in Scripture represents testing, preparation, and transformation. What will your next forty days look like? Continue walking with God as He writes your next chapter.

Remember: You are not alone. You are not forgotten. You are not without hope.

You are being led, loved, and lifted—day by day—by a God who sees you, hears you, and calls you His own.

With love and gratitude,
Louis & Kiera

"I can do all things through Christ who strengthens me" Phil. 4:13

ABOUT THE AUTHORS

Louis and Kiera DesChamps are passionate communicators, ministry leaders, and lifelong servants in their local church and community. Married for over thirty-two years, Louis and Kiera bring a lived-in faith and grounded hope to everything they do—both in life and in this devotional.

Louis is a veteran of the United States Air Force, known for his servant heart, storytelling, and a gift for encouragement that resonates with every generation. Kiera is a speaker, trainer, and mentor, known for her ability to weave truth and humor with authenticity and grace. Together, they've ministered in family, youth, and women's ministries, equipping others with the tools to walk faithfully through seasons of transition, grief, restoration, and growth.

Forty Days and Forty Nights was born from more than three decades of preaching, teaching, and lived experiences. With each devotional entry, they've poured in Scripture, personal reflection, and hope for readers walking through their own wilderness seasons.

Louis and Kiera believe in being about His business and sharing their stories with as many as will listen. They are living the very prayers they once prayed and are forever grateful to God for it.

They currently live in North Carolina, where they continue to serve and grow in ministry together. They are the proud parents of two sons and the overjoyed Nonna and PoppO to two granddaughters who keep them laughing and grounded in love.

Favorite Scripture:

"But as it is written:
Eye has not seen, nor ear heard,
Nor have entered into the heart of man
The things which God has prepared for those who love Him."'

—1 Corinthians 2:9 (NKJV)

Connect with Louis and Kiera DesChamps

To book Louis and Kiera to speak at your church,
faith-based organization, couples retreat, or conference:

Email: kd@kdconsults.com

Let's connect on social media:

LinkedIn: https://www.linkedin.com/in/kieradeschamps

TikTok: https://www.tiktok.com/@kdconsults

If you are a fan of this book, please tell others...

- Write about *Forty Days and Forty Nights* on your blog, e-magazine, company newsletter, and social media channels.
- Feature Louis and Kiera DesChamps as guests on your podcast or radio/TV broadcast.
- Write an authentic, positive review on Amazon.com.
- Post on your social media channels.
- Purchase additional copies for your church and faith-based organizations.

www.ingramcontent.com/pod-product-compliance
Lightning Source LLC
Chambersburg PA
CBHW051519120626
46551CB00012B/998